The Road Less Travel:
The Road Warrior

The Road Less Travel:
The Road Warrior

Life as a road chapter

Anthony Ruben Lee

To order additional copies of this book, contact:
Xlibris Corporation
1-888-795-4274
www.Xlibris.com
Orders@Xlibris.com
92452

This book is dedicated to those who are struggling within themselves in their mind, body, and soul during their Christian walk, having fears of the unknown. You are not alone. Jesus Christ is with you in every step of the way till your breaking point starts. I tell you that you are the light of the world, that you have a message to give to them. With the real me in this book, with words from heaven, and with my first book going public, there will be mixed emotions. Some will love it; some will not. Who cares, when you hear from God from a different side you will appreciate.

Thank you dad for teaching me the ways of Christ and your love and understanding and wisdom forever your son, my dad, forever HECTOR J. LARIZ

And for my mother also for your love and for believing in me every step of the way your drive and determination forever your son, my mother forever DEBORAH LEE LARIZ

The More I Pray

The more joy of the Lord is my strength
The more I fight for what is mine
The more I can stand on his promises
The more to let my light shine before men
The more watching and praying without season
The more I love your tender mercies
The more I want to see Jesus's face
You are the water of life so fill me up, Lord this is my prayer
to you.

The More I Pray

The more I am on fire for the Lord
The more powerful the hit in the devil's face
The more I swing the sword of righteousness
The greater the spiral expectations it is
The more spiral blessings fall down
There will be no more crying
There will not be any more laws and rules to follow by.
There will be more freedom to rule and reign with the saints
of God.

The More I Pray

The more I decrease
The more he increases
The more I move in his voice
The more I kill the flesh to revive my soul
The more I train myself to be fearless
The more I say the Lord is my strength
To my last breath, the more I want to see Jesus

*a*s an inheritance from heaven above and from the Bible, the words have taught our hearts to rise. Ties, with unity to an uncorrupted body under no evil, fading into the clouds so high that all saints of all races are empowered by God. We are kept in his arms of salvation. We walk by faith as strangers here, but Christ shall call us home. The Lord said in his Word in Isaiah 61:1-2: 1.The spirit of the lord God is upon me; because the lord hath anointed me to preach good tidings unto the meek; he hath sent me to bind up the brokenhearted, to proclaim liberty to the captives, and the opening of the prison to them that are bound; 2. To proclaim the acceptable year of the lord, and the day of vengeance of our god; to comfort all that mourn." Have you become the enemy of the state? You have been predestined, purchased, postproduction, and been remodeled by the Maker's hand. Is this you, my son, my daughter? My deepest fears in myself leaps out like an empty tunnel screaming out in the top of my voice, asking myself, the half of me has the passion for it but the other side say.

I do not want to share this with everybody, with everyone else. I do not have to offer this gift to this group of people. The question is can this take me to my breaking point? Do I have a future to look forward to? There are subjects of life that come up. Where is God calling you? Out of hiding, yes, he is teaching me. He's a voice that I can yield to my spirit, hungry and thirsty, just like we yield to flesh.

When he does that to me, I am the true Christian. The true self shows up, comes out. Jesus, he, is keeping me. I am getting better with love of him in my heart. As the years go by, I am still standing on his promises. We see what the devil does. We can foresee the devil. We see what he can do. We are not alone. There are people praying for us, fighting the battle together. If one of us gets hurt, the whole body hurts. We all want to go to the finish line.

We keep our arms up, with crushed fist, ready to fight all the time. We need to keep our arms down and let god do the fighting to grasp the holy spirit to grasp more fire more zeal for who you are the true self so God can move through you.

I'm trying to focus on my prayerful life, focus on my life. Where am I going from here? My small story in this big world that which I'm living in God in all his ways he wants to be with you if you can think about it stop whatever you are doing stop for a second or two in your day Just think to yourself, *What is the purpose of my life while life itself is going away right before my eyes, and I am unable to see clearly the changes and series of things that I do not have control of?*

Flipping through the pages of the chapters of my life and thinking back, I realize God has my pages of chapters of life. Yes, it is good to think about it, but who has plans for your life? I know that it seems so far off from you, not answering your prayers. There is no need to find him. He is there where you need him all the time, a willing heart, a humble meek vessel Jesus Christ. He will give you plans to do this week, next week, next month, and next year. We need to listen to his voice. Our heart and soul should be listening to his voice, what to do next, right now, a plan of action. The crossroads is this: We keep on searching for the Stone Age crossroads of life and can't believe that it is happening to us. The decision is this: We put our set right field person into a rock and a hard place and safe place. There are periods of time very unpredictable the gods economy how deep can you go between the Christian view and the world view myths we use hellos as loop holes deceitfulness acts in church of acts in the world and putting them in the same level together one foot in and one foot out.

Leaving our understanding of the past, now in the present, we know we have to go through things of life that had to happen. We all go through the circle of life. We all have stories when you hit rock bottom. What is your passion? What makes you keep on going? It is plan, which makes you tick. You are striving to his higher calling. Do you know who's calling you?

The fear of the Lord is beginning of wisdom. Trust in the Lord with all your heart. You are born for a purpose. It is time to go forward. There is something powerful from God yet to come learning of his will makes you more understanding of his plan.

We can be as great people for the Lord's mind's eyes. We all want to be one of the fuels for the human race. They only lack the light to show the way as vassals sent by Jesus Christ. For this reason above all, for our complexity of sin, God sent his only son to die for our sins. For that, we can keep his legacy alive forever and ever. It is he who gives you liberty, freedom; the real liberty comes from God. The Christian walk of my life is about running to my daddy, my God, my Lord, and Savior, walking by faith. It is very important to remember, speaking by faith to receive, God's promises for you.

I know you are saying to yourself, "Here goes another book on spiritual lies. I'm going to be wasting my time reading one of those books. I am not here to teach you. I am here in this book, trying to relate to guide you with the same problems we face in an everyday life." The basic and basis is to find ourselves in a tight spot sometimes—the only one who can teach you the right way is Jesus Christ himself. Has all your prayers been answered? You are free to walk in the light.

We need to protect our spirit, our soul, man, from evil thinking, doing evil things, saying evil stuff. I put my flesh to death. We should tie up and put it under our feet. Now where do you stand with God? We are people with a purpose. This can be a tag team match. What is your stronghold? Your mind, your body, your past, your future, which one? Tell God everything, your deepest fears little by little, step-by-step. It will come together in due time. God is setting it all up, for the big story of my life in ministry with God is that.

When you first begin to minister, you pray and pray and pray. When you are ready, you go out and minister. You pour out yourself in every way. You fight to listen to God, to know what he wants you to do. Then after you finish, you crash. The devil comes, and all too often, he wins. We fall in some way. We get angry at those around us, or we lax, thinking that we have done some great thing. Then Satan comes and steals what God has done in us. The way to protect our selves from this happening is to develop endurance.

Endurance brings two things into the life of the believer. First, it brings a determination that no matter how high we come to, we still have the emotional energy left to continue fighting after the victory.

The second thing that endurance brings is the ability to fight any time, any place, no matter what we need, to develop our endurance so that we will always have what it takes to defeat the enemy. Wherever he shows his ugly head, go on, keep fighting. You will win. What is your motivation in that saying? Are you built for change? Are you ready for a 100 percent? All of you in a network, the best result is to live by the Word of God, the nature of God, the love to give like Jesus Christ gave his life for our sins.

Love can go the extra mile. The real Christian can go beyond forever. You got to learn to sacrifice yourself for the sake of others. Learn to be the last in this world, but we will be first in the kingdom of heaven.

The mind of Christ is faster than that of the natural man. He can remember who you are. You do not want to see your blessing just pass you by. You just got to see it grow right before your eyes, sometimes without you knowing. Keep your eyes on your goal. We are serving a great God. We are sons and daughters after gods on heart in saying this some shall depart from the faith and some do not see the whole picture what is your position with yourself and Jesus Christ carrying out the true obedience we are born to be leaders.

Be concentrated. Inspect your foundation. Be real. Don't show fake love to people. Be in perfect harmony. With the truth, you have to touch God's wisdom, understanding to be aware of some of the things all around you and your actions.

We all make mistakes with our month. You have to be 110 percent and over beyond with your God. Trust in him. Be fruitful and multiply. Have dominion over the fish of the sea in your life, the world within you. The test will come.

A test proves the true value of true fullness. Test comes to our life to help us think more clearly, to think things through. Are you ready for the next test? Are you ready for the next spiritual level? How long are you going to carry your cross. Be still. The voice of the Lord is talking to you. We have forgotten the words of Jesus. In time, we will not doubt God with our doubting hearts. So say help me, Lord, to love you again. Renew the fire again after that. It is like a spiritual wake-up call slap after you been throw hell and high water raise up cry out to the lord understanding who you are today.

Psalms 139:15-18

[15] My substance was not hid from thee, when I was made in secret, and curiously wrought in the lowest parts of the earth.

[16] Thine eyes did see my substance, yet being imperfect; and in thy book all my members were written, which in continuance were fashioned, when as yet there was none of them.

[17] How precious also are thy thoughts unto me, O GOD! How great is the sum of them!

[18] If I should count them, they are more in number than the sand: when I awake, I am still with thee.

Have the mind of Christ take off your old clothes. Put on your new clothes. In the new testament of your life, keep on standing on his promises. A state of mind is a state of attitude. You have to look beyond your own self. You are set apart from the world for the masters use hands raised with praise offerings and surrendering to God. Walk in the Word. Walk and pray day and night. Don't refuse the Word of God. Don't refuse the voice of the Lord. Stay hot for the Lord. You have been Branded for life. The seed of Jesus Christ is to be planted in your life. Dare to say it. I have living hope. God is always on the move for you. He is waiting on you. Do not forget his ways. You are a masterpiece from God. Be in perfect harmony in Jesus. 1 Thessalonians 5:14-22 says this. Now we exhort you, brethren, warn them that are unruly, comfort the feebleminded, support the weak, be patient toward all men. 16. Rejoice evermore. 17. Pray without ceasing. 18. In every thing give thanks: for this is the will of God in Christ Jesus concerning you. no fighting, no glory.

Hebrews 12:1-3. 1. Wherefore seeing we also are compassed about with so great a cloud of witnesses, let us lay aside every weight, and the sin which doth so easily beset us, and let us run with patience the race that is set before us. 2. Looking unto Jesus the author and finisher of our faith; who for the joy that was set before him endured the cross, despising the shame, and is set down at the right hand of the throne of God. 3. For consider him that endured such contradiction of sinners against himself, lest ye be wearied and faint in your minds. Your heart got to be right with God all the time. Be like Jesus. Walk, talk, and act. Respond to different things of life. Watch what you are seeing in your daily living. Don't do. Don't let things that are bad cling to you. Psalm 101:2-3. 2. I will behave myself wisely in a perfect way. O when wilt thou come unto me? I will walk within my house with a perfect heart. 3. I will set no wicked thing before mine eyes: I hate the work of them that turn aside; it shall not cleave to me. Take a stand today. What do you believe in? What are the most talked about subjects in your daily living, in the workplace, in the grocery store, in the mall, at the park, at school, your neighbors, your home church?

We lost something very important and dear to us. It is our own personal inventory. Our souls feel free to talk to Christian believers about what's weighing heavy on our hearts.

Today we tend to keep it to ourselves and keeping our mouth shut in church, but we go out. We do what we want, so we do it anyway. Revelation 3:20-22 says. 20. Behold, I stand at the door, and knock: if any man hear my voice, and open the door, I will come in to him, and will sup with him, and he with me. 21. To him that overcometh will I grant to sit with me in my throne, even as I also overcame, and am set down with my Father in his throne. 22. He that hath an ear, let him hear what the Spirit saith unto the churches. Psalm 51:10-12.says. 10. Create in me a clean heart, O God; and renew a right spirit within me. 11. Cast me out away from thy presence; and take not thy Holy Spirit from me. 12. Restore unto me the joy of thy salvation; and uphold me with thy free spirit. 13. Then will I teach transgressors thy ways; and sinners shall be converted unto thee. 2 Corinthians 4:15-16. This verse is about daily living, learning to live day by day. 15. For all things are for your sakes, that the abundant grace might through the thanksgiving of many redound to the glory of God. 16. For which cause we faint not; but though our outward man perish, yet the inward man is renewed day by day. I want to rest in his glory. I want to be blessed in the anointing. Don't let the devil make a nest in your soul. I thrust myself to you. I lean not to my own understanding, but I lean on Gods understanding in the midst of my troubles, and when I am falling, lord you pick me up, and put me back on my spiritual walk, and put me back in your arms. I can stand in all of you. Jesus, I've forgotten the words that you had spoken to me. Forgive me for my unbelief. Renew the fire again. I have taken journeys that have drawn me far from you. Now I am returning to your ever-flowing mercies. I bow my heart before you in the goodness of your presence, your grace forever shining like a beacon in the night. Anything I say, anything I do with Jesus' help, I will I stand for what I believe. I will be more of a help to someone who needs help. Not my will, let your will from heaven above be a witness for all to get the understanding, so break off those chains of things of this world. Break off all that the flesh wants. After you did all you could, just give it to Jesus. Ephesians 6:10-19.says. 10. Finally, my brethren, be strong in the Lord, and in the power of his might. 11. Put on the whole armour of God, that ye may be able to stand against the wiles of the devil. 12. For we wrestle not against flesh and blood, but against principalities, against powers, against the rulers of the darkness of this world, against spiritual wickedness in high places. 13. Wherefore take unto you the whole armour of God, that ye may be able to withstand in the evil day, and having done all, to stand. 14. Stand therefore, having your loins girt about with truth, and having on the breastplate of righteousness. 15. And your feet shod with the preparation of the gospel of peace; 16. Above all, taking the shield of faith, wherewith ye shall be able to quench all the fiery darts of the wicked. 17. And take the helmet of salvation, and the sword of the Spirit, which is the word of God: 18. Praying always with all prayer and supplication in the Spirit, and watching thereunto with all perseverance and supplication for all saints. 19. And for me, that utterance may be given unto me, that I may open my mouth boldly, to make known the mystery of the gospel. Let Jesus guide your steps. With this, comes the devil who tries to throw a curveball in your life. If you are not aware what's going on around you, is it your choice to give in or not to give in? Matthew 26:41 says. 41. Watch and pray, that ye enter not into temptation: the spirit indeed is willing, but the flesh is weak. Can you find yourself in him? He is setting on his throne, watching you every day of your life. He is not lost. We learn how far God knows everything. He is God of the universe. God, in his infinite glory and infinite power and wisdom, the author and finisher, he knows the being and the ending, directing all the universal and the stars limitless, tremendous and, saying all of this takes care of God's business, and he will take care of your business it's already done for you. Obedience is the road to a wonderful adventures with the Lord, adventures that you have not lived before. Wicked men obey from fear; good people obey from love. It is time to get busy obeying God. Just go and see what he has for you: faith, hope, determination running through your inner most being. I am saying to the Lord. I am using this body that you have given me to be put to the test for your glory. I know without a shadow of a doubt that there is a blessing waiting for me, design to my needs.

As long as a person doesn't know what he doesn't know, he will not grow. I know what I don't know, so the secret of success in life is for a man to be ready for his time when it comes. Think about every move you make always on the edge of the cliff with the devil causing you to do stuff. Romans 8:25-28 says. 25. But if we hope for that we see not, then do we with patience wait for it. 26. Likewise the Spirit also helpeth our infirmities: for we know not what we should pray for as we ought: but the Spirit itself maketh intercession for us with groanings which cannot be uttered. 27. And he that searcheth the hearts knoweth what is the mind of the Spirit, because he maketh intercession for the saints according to the will of God. 28. And we know that all things work together for good to them that love God, to them who are the called according to his purpose. Philippians 4:19. 19. But my God shall supply all your need according to his riches in glory by Christ Jesus. Let God's love rule and rain in your life, and stop thinking so loosely. Take hold of yourself, and tell the devil, "not today. So grab, hold on God's thoughts let Jesus, take over. Just remember, no limits. Do not be one of those single-minded persons. Do you know your own identity? Are you free from yourself? What is causing your driving force within to discover the true natural gift from God. 1 Peter 2:9-10 says. 9. But ye are a chosen generation, a royal priesthood, an holy nation, a peculiar people; that ye should shew forth the praises of him who hath called you out of darkness into his marvelous light. 10. Which in time past were not a people, but are now the people of God: which had not obtained mercy, but now have obtained mercy. Be in the mind-set of the box but always thinking beyond the box. Proverbs 3:6-8. 6. In all thy ways acknowledge him, and he shall direct thy paths. 7. Be not wise in thine own eyes: fear the Lord, and depart from evil. 8. It shall be health to thy navel, and marrow to thy bones. Living up to his promises every day of your life, asking yourself, "What is the solution of living a sinful life?" You can change, and you will change to the next level as my heart is heavy with God's love inside of you. That makes me fall to my knees, living up to the challenge. To find the grace that has surrounded me all my life to keep going like I did, I keep grace very close to me. With God's help, we can catch. He has spirit; he has vision for this human race who is searching for realization in their struggles.

As I look around, I see people every day who look like they are really struggling with a lot of stuff. You see it in their walk, their face, their eyes, the way they move wildly. You walk through all this. You just see what Jesus sees like a set of spiritual binoculars. How can you find yourself in all the crazy things of life? Can we move in his perfect will? To show fourth your presents for all can see. I search for holiness. You must consider this: He is waiting on us to wake up to the truth in you that the blueprint of God's love for you and your future is to be the one that will not bend or bow for no one. The unmovable not shaking, a soul stared up for your thirst for his words that he has spoken for two thousand years that all have been blinded to the truth. There are many threats on our way of life, and not all of them are uniformed, and nor do we carry guns. We must not waver on our own feelings. This is not a scientific theory but a spiritual theory. Are you in good standing with Jesus? Confession is already in the making to show our way of freedom right now. We are fighting for souls every day of our life. We must not throw bricks. The most dangerous thing you should not do is to stop a man who has determination to do something about it; whatever the problem is, you must be able to deny flesh to become reborn in Christ. Your mind, body, and your very soul will all change, and now it is a supernatural strength that comes all over you. You must block this world from your eyes to find out. Things are not what they seem to be. You need to know you are a stranger in a foreign land. You are not alone. There are believers like you with the some zeal. That fire burns in your soul in sight of us. A life to live, to live in God's world, you find new things in him, but most of all, to talk to him, feel his presence, feel his love, feel his peace, feel his Holy Spirit. The one thing we must do is fill our hearts with his holy presence. Let the living waters flow. You are drinking from the heavenly waters. It is poured out upon you so that Jesus Christ can manifest his healing, reconstructing, putting your life together, restoring, but this time you will be prepared. Your soul inspired by reading his words, getting some good teaching not that fake stuff continually day by day devotion praying talking to god the one that has blessed you through the good times and the bad times.

He is the best friend you will ever have. He will be there for you always. You must be prayed up at all time's, on your knees, crying out. Just lift up your hands to him. It is the very core of you, the true you. If you are still reading this book so far you, are getting the message. So come with me through this journey, and together we both can find some kind of an answer. I do not claim to have all the answers, but this is one of them. At times, it does not seem you feel things like other people feel. You are different from the rest, a horse of a different color who has all the weight on his shoulders. When times get tuff, who has the gift from God?

Who is standing for what they believe in they are called "Jesus freaks for life yes the ones that can stand in the middle of a busy shopping mall with lots of people all around at the food court at the video games place, anything you can think of groups of Christians sharing the love of Jesus. Everything I ever needed comes from God, so you are looking for something that can come close to him, so you counterfeit to your liking. So, you go alone with where ever the wind takes you, not knowing that you went off the road with your Lord, not having your soul grounded in him. So pick up your broken pieces of your soul on the side of the road, like road kill. Talking about Jesus, he can do anything I need. Jesus plans not my plans. I tell, you know, as I speak to you in this book. There are Christians fighting with the devil with all heart and soul. The devil crept up in their mind. Throughout life, they are struggling with things that they just shook off from their past. It is dealing with them in their present time.

How can we fight this windfall in our lives today? Some people find it very easy. For some, it takes years. There are learning processes for both, by telling the Lord, "What are you doing in my life? Do you care about me? I am asking a question are you losing me lord I have the faith but where in my life and when can I start to hear your voice I want to see and feel different. How will I get there? Why me? What are you saying to me? Time is short, so stop wondering and stop trying to figure it out. As soon as you figure it out, it is time to die. Sometimes in your life, it is like a SOS. Real personnel prayer. You will be with God. I remember some things that I did not want to remember, just to know that I am stronger than ever in my heart and soul, to stay forever. He is my source of strength, he is my source of peace in Christ, the Lord.

I will stand in faith that God will supply all my needs according to his riches and glory for his name sake in saying that the right time all you need is to get up and move going out with boldness in the right path for your blessings are coming closer than you think. While I am on my knees Jesus puts the puzzles, and pieces of your broken heart back together again he has the blueprints of your life so give your problems to him he will give you peace let god help you out you can pray and read the Bible better than that, stop sizing yourself get in shape with Jesus.

Make that plan happen. He will help your marriage, your money, and your health. He will show you that he can do things, therefore back up to see what it is. Quit second-guessing. God stands by his Word, God gives a sound mind. It is time to go through the journey. Somehow, someway, you have to know Jesus gave up his blood, gave everything. When you understand that, be ready for him. For the cause of Christ, get on your knees. Be like him, not pretending to be like him kill the flesh by fasting and build up the spirit man up out of you in the perfect will of God. In a promise, in prayer, lord you are always here with me. You are always there completely and constantly everywhere. You are all I ever need. It never leaves my soul, Lord. These hands are open, Lord Jesus, take them. You are the only one who can draw me here. When I come clean, I can't pretend to any fake thing in me. Wash me in your love. The shadows of my past life start falling behind me, and hope begins to rise in my soul.

Make me a living witness, a living vassal. You open my eyes to the truth. Nothing can explain how I feel right now. It is a burning sanction like fire in my heart, that confirmation, that support when you are really grounded in him. This is the reason why I pray, to draw myself to him, to get clear understanding. Thanking god for making away of getting my life started and for what's inside of me branded stamped framed set in place by the makers hand deep inside my soul all the evil stuff I used to do are gone.

We are fighting a never-ending battle, trying to destroy this flash to bring up a renewed, reborn spirit man. While we are on the subject of our souls, when we try to burn our sinful worldly stuff? I mean really burn that little demon nagging at you, lighting up a match with some lighter fluid and trying to burn it up. For example, it could be for some people. Drugs, music, porn movies, and sex magazines and then your car, your house, your job, your money. All of this and more take you away from God's plans for you, for some people. They go too far and wind up in the mental institutions or the grave. So choose who you are going to serve: Jesus Christ or the devil. Do not sell your soul to the devil. That is the most dangerous thing to do. Maybe in some cases, people do not understand you. They run all over you, forgive and ask god to help you but excuse me, I am trying to do something for my Lord and savior. That I have been sealed by the maker's hand from heaven. Nothing else can express my gratitude to sacrifice. All of you got the key, think about it. He has everything for you, so reach out and grab it. Seek after him. Get close to his holy presence. Nobody can understand you. They are on a different level in Christ. You are a different person from them, but you are getting there. He's helping you. He has a voice, his presence is all around you. Like surround stereo, he is touching you in ways you have never been touched before by his spirit. Are you ready to learn from the Lamb of God to maintain a teachable spirit always willing to learn wisdom, that wisdom is calling you out to understand his ways? You got to know where you stand.

God treats us like fellow soldiers. Be wise. Trust in God. He is trying to tell you not to be lowly. He advises Christians to be above the normal. Be like as (John 7:38) says, he that believe on me, as the scripture hath said, out his belly shall flow rivers of living waters. Be of good cheer. You can speak well in front of others. The words will come. As a matter of fact, it is already in you. The spirit of the Lord drops a seed in you. It is called his spirit in your soul. The moment you give your life to God, the plan of God has already begun. On the day you were born, your first breath of life went to him. He will give you peace. With that peace comes this, like when you go to sleep for a while, after walking with him and getting to know him he will wake you up in the middle of the night when you just getting into a deep sleep, and in the stillness of the night, it comes out, a voice or a shaking of the bed not in a forceful way, but in a way he knows just what it takes to wake you up he knows how you sleep so what happens next is it.

Your choice is to wake up and start praying. That's right. Hit the knees, or stay in your bed, opening your eyes. When you hear the voice of God after you close your eyes, have you had something like this happen to you? Maybe not, it did to me so you know this part about you. So get cleaned up with in yourself. You got to be absolutely concentrated frequently in tune with Jesus, so be totally sold out for Jesus. Give him praises. And the most important thing you must do is read the Bible that is your sword, to fight the devil with whatever it takes. Get out your element to search for higher calling in life. Believe in yourself in your heart and soul get it inside of you that is the extreme way to go. At this point, I have to tell you something, It is a little deep. So like this today, something sparked that hiding place inside my mind, the deepest part of my soul, a new chapter. I really dough deep with this one it is not my future it is not present it is about the unfinished business of my past you keep on going over and over that scene, wondering if I could have done it better. I knew that I was different from the other kids around me. Every day, it felt like I was floating through my childhood on a cloud, going through the emotions, stretching out my hands, trying to do something like I was not there at all. The devil stole my innocence. When I was thirteen, I saw things I was not supposed to see. I did things to see what would happen. This is my darkest secret ever in my life. This is why I am writing this kind of book it's for that reason. I want to help other Christians or non-Christians if they want to pick up this book. This is one of the sources to find out the truth that Christians do struggle with sin. So, I am just a voice throughout the masses. I know God's voice, and he knows me. To build on that Jesus is my best friend that's what kind of relationship you got to have to be blessed by god this is my vow that I have inside of me that I will not bow down to no other gods are so call gods it does not make any sense to pray to a empty idol.

They make it so hard for themselves on that side, but on Jesus Christ's side, his way is made easy. He is the true light he want's all of you not half of you. You said a simple little prayer when you first got saved. When you did that, you got all access paid by and through the blood of Jesus Christ. There is something to tell the world about the peace you have. He is building a solid foundation in you. He is meant to love you. He will change your worldview, saying to yourself, "I can see clearly now." It is the way he looks at you. I do not want to puff up myself. I left up the name of Jesus with all my soul full of prosperity this is not a pretzel little prayer this is big to me God is trying to tell you there is a promise birth inside of you for a long time so when it is time count it all joy and peace and sweet rest in the lord.

Be ready at all times. Keep on sharpening your sword, my brother and sister in Christ. You have to tell about the bloodstain cross of Jesus, everything in your life, in your soul that he came to give you internal life forever more. You must walk with him daily, to sunup, to sundown. His will never fades away. Keep seeking his face, humbling yourself, praise his holy name. You got to understand no matter what people say to you, move on god's word it is true. You have to trust on that for the rest of your life, you must prevent yourself from falling in to sin. Your soul will open to anything. Many great temptations can be very damaging to your soul, your vision with out the Holy

Spirit, for the Lord has to be clear to work in you. Keep your focus, your five senses that is called your common sense that God gave you. He holds the blueprint of your entire life. You got to know this, your deepest desire, your weakness, and your strengths, so call on him so that he can deliver you from the follies of the devil. Say it to yourself. Kill this flesh, Lord Jesus. You will start to look like the maker from the inside out. He will give you favor with people in high places. You will go to places you have not been before. Some things you will understand; some things you will not.

So he will capture you with his voice like a best friend. He gave it all to you to get access to internal life. Be ready at all times. He is the pathfinder. Choose what path to take for your life today. Jesus is the one who can make your way trust in him. You can feel him right smack in the middle of your chest. Jesus Christ is grabbing you. It is like he stuck his hands in the middle of your chest, cracking it up, turning left and right, tugging at your very heart and soul. Could it be that God himself is trying to talk to you that you are doing something wrong. Maybe you need to pray more. Read your Bible more. You are speeding high. Slow yourself down. What is it that is causing you to react that way? You need to lay it all at the altar, a sacrifice of praise. He only can give you peace, a sweet rest. We need to lift up the standards of God in our life today, to understand his ways. What is your calling? Many of us became church mice, and your comfort zones those lukewarm Christians lacking all sense of direction.

Do not know who you are. So what are you going to do, my friend? You are reading this book for a reason? It is God's plan to change your life. You can't see it now. You will just go through your life. Daily struggles will lose their power over us. When we realize that all these things we are going through are a part of God's plan for our lives, we realize that he is wise beyond our comprehension and knows exactly what we need each and every day. Jesus said that he would pour out the Holy Spirit upon those who would come to him and drink his living water, which not only quenches our thirst, but also flows out, as a river of life to bless the lives of those around us. This is the reason why we are on this earth. I am talking about those Christians who have been saved and filled with his Holy Spirit and those who have been down that same road, and now your whole life has been changed for the better. You are a different person now than six months ago than one year ago are even five, to ten, or even twenty years ago and still learning new things every day.

And please do not be a part of the rat race, meeting deadlines, rushing to be the next success story. You are fighting a losing battle with the world's ethics of doing things you are supposed to do and not doing them, but with one hand you are losing your peace of mind, not taking time-out praying or just saying thank you Jesus for another day of living. One moment you are standing by the seashore, looking out at that blue clear water, looking at the sunset just beyond the horizon, just having a nice day. Let God mold you and shape you in his image. It doesn't matter what's going on around me. I am going to be a true living vessel for Christ. I want to help somebody in need. For some people, they have to learn the hard way, not the easy way or God's way. So it is your choice to choose who you are going to believe. Stop hanging around narrow-minded people. Your faith lies in Jesus Christ and in nothing else.

And sometimes it seems like a little twist of fate at one point in your life, at the specific place, date, and time. That is a call to meet God's plan for your life, and that is called the blueprint coming in to play. It is not *déjà vu*, and you are thinking to yourself, "Have I been here before now?" So go on. Don't stop. Keep going on. Quit fighting with yourself. Jesus is with you, not against you. Now you are asking yourself. "Ok God why me? Could you choose somebody else for the job, not today not this month or this year for a time such as this?" For the things that are coming, one of these days, you are going to make a stand toward the devil and has evil works, and now step back out of this book, If it's only you or other people around look around, what do you see? You may be thinking to yourself, "I can change people's lives from the things I know from God."

I have faith in you, Jesus. I want to be a successful Christian, doing God's business. With that, he will take care of me and my family. What are your deepest fears, or have you gone far enough in life to prove it to yourself, you are so slow and lazy, to complete one area in your life, to make it over to the other side of life? I am at the end of my rope. I have to make a choice, do it my own way, or God's way. I have gone through so many nights and days and even months struggling with myself. I do things that a normal person wouldn't do, and some people are trying to teach you about your own life. At the time when every heart is in trouble, everything is a mass up inside you. I do not want to know what's going on in their world affairs at that time, for you to have a quiet moment to reflect, relax, and to realize why God is really talking to me. I do exist. This is important to me. First priority is to talk to Jesus about everything, even considering your future. You are searching in your mind for a solution. Quit second-guessing yourself.

And now, you are trying to get ahead in life. Half your lifetime, and the wheels of time keep going. Can you swim, not letting other people twist you around? By this time, all these things that you care about are putting you under water. Now you are drowning. Can you see your way out through the not-so-clear waters? You need to come up to the surface, to the brink, and wake up from a dream state. Are you ready to move to the next level? The Lord Jesus Christ has been so good to you, and he has been there for you all your life when you needed him the most. Just remember that you are a blessing to yourself, and he's around you every day. And your family will be coming back together for a purpose at such a time as this when your gifts will get stronger. As you get closer and closer to him, your Maker keeps on encouraging each and every one of you. In time, just be patient. The time will come, and you will know it when you have been through some trying times. When the biggest weights of life come on to all of you, you feel like throwing in the towel, and you are all by yourself. You must stir up the gift in you, and all of a sudden, happiness starts to well up in your heart and soul. It is a voice saying, "You can do it." You should get up and say, "Yes, Lord." Now you know what causes you to fall into this, and you encourage yourself and other people around you.

Just be patient. The time will come. Just wait for it, and you will know it. We all have been through some trying times. You felt like quitting. You are not yourself, and then the things inside of you like happiness, peace, hope, and faith in you starts to come alive you can do it. The devil is a liar. God is working on my behalf, so saying it to yourself, "He is going to take care of the problem. "Lord I know you will provide for my family, so what's next? You have done some sins. You sugarcoated that white stuff that is called "icing on the cake." for this time of your life some things are not what it seems always checking things out all around you is it real or fake you know what's going on outside but you can't find out what's going on with the inside man so who's doing the talking here.

I do not want to see sin or hear sin in order to protect what is valuable to me. My very own virtues do I have what it takes to give someone the basic truths about my Jesus that has the capability to know the truth you have opened up my eyes and my heart you are healing me to know the truth. The truth of the matter is, can you really trust yourself anymore? You ask the question to yourself. You have been on this same road before. You can make it hard for yourself or easy. Your choices are the drums of life beating you up. Have they stopped for you, and when they stopped, did you feel the peace of God all over? You can actually feel the winds of change in the air. And now, you are focused. Do not count on friends. Count on your family. Be in close ties with them. Let Jesus Christ talk to you if you are not free inside. I am talking about your very heart and soul. Count on joy. There is one thing I can tell you. I have made my decision. I have staked my claim. I have drawn a line in the sand, and I'll not be ashamed. With the world behind me, and the cross before me, by the grace of God, I will serve the Lord.

I know things right now are tight for you. There is not enough time to read the Bible or pray. Yes, pray. I am just real with you and your fast life. Do not put God on your to-do list of things. This should come automatically to you, but it does not. Sometimes, you have been tired and stretched to your limits. Maybe you are not a toy soldier. You are a real, unbreakable soldier. You can stand any kind of weather. Do not draw apart from god. Stay connected to the Lord like you do with the IPhone or the IPad, for the generation out there. Talking understanding for the purpose of the mission is very important so get up and dust yourself off and pick up your sword. You are trying to face your own problems and your fears. How you are going to handle every day of your life is the first thing you face in the morning. When you open your eyes, the first deep breaths just before you rise your body up from the bed, the movement of your body is all guided by God himself. Do not lock yourself from God. He knows your pet sins.

And oh, by the way, you are the king of excuses, for every time you go to a church, you talk lies in a group and you know they are spirit filled people that reads there Bible every day. Stop playing games, your life will be cut off. You are praying for lost souls. Let me just be real with this, just you think about that. Are you a die-hard Christian or an easygoing Christian? The choice is yours. Wake up and smell the coffee, or your energy drink. Are you filling up your soul with food? I mean the Bible. It is one way to God. What's going on inside of me? I devise my own behavior. We have a long way to go. We all are trying to be the best for Jesus, and the devil, we can see him from a long way. Before he gets to your personal space, your mind, body, and soul, you will get it. Take your time. Your Lord will guide you step-by-step. Yes, you are a walking dead man and woman. I really hate this. You are trying to do God's works, and your second person starts to talk to you. At the same time, your inside starts to fight for what is right; it is rumbling commotion going on. There are lots of condemning thoughts. It is like being back in the biblical days when they stoned people to death. It is because they have committed a big sin. They have been caught in the act or someone saw them take something that did not belong to them, so they got stoned to death.

Now this explains how you are going through this part of your life. It does feel that there are lots of people stoning you to death, you are dealing with issues so you cover it up so there you go back in the lab again trying to cover up your sin so you have a lot of love to give out, not realizing there are people looking up to you, so straighten up your upper lip straighten up your tie, comb your hair, right young solider Gods got your back. You got to remember that not all people are ready for this kind of contact. Spiral training, believe it or not, you can overdo yourself. You can get what they call "spiral stress" in body, mind, and soul. You can be the die-hard Christian with a vengeance, and at the same time, you may be feeding the homeless or helping the staff at the old folks' home you need to rest to see the big difference. So understand who you are. God does not worry. He will give you peace about everything. We cannot hold a torch to light another's path without brightening our own. We are so cold and away from things that can penetrate our feelings.

Define what is real to you. Do you know who you are? What makes you are breaks you not feeling the rhythm of life calling for technical support or will you be the land mark to gain back for what the devil took from you. Oh please do be a hallmark story another poor soul has been taking again what makes me so different saying why me lord am I so different from the next guy, oh God make my heart as stone cold person you do not know what you are saying acting on pure desperation you know God does not work like that, and stop putting things out of contexts. It is because you're hearing those cry's going to hell. Even the ones who are living with you can see it in their eyes, in the way they do certain tasks, the way they eat and sleep. These are the only basic details. It goes on for more than that. You have to be in God's perfect will. His plan for your life, those dreams you have been having for a long time all kinds, long and short dreams, some of those, can happen next year, next month, next week, tomorrow, or even today at a certain time and place. Now it is up to you. Where do you line up? Only time will tell.

You can fight the flash. Be a part of God's world tell me something. Are you right now sad, happy, peaceful, joyful, lonely, or you just thinking about tomorrow, I do not know what my future holds. Are you telling the devil let's make a deal? I do not think you want to do that. Quit finding quick solutions. You need to wait on God for your answers. Are you causing yourself a voice traffic jam between the devil and the lord get tune in on the right frequency? Jesus Christ stays in the safe zone, not in the dead zone. You are struggling with both worlds: the Christian life and the worldly life. Your spirit is fighting with your flesh. The bad side is telling you to keep your worldly goods. The good side of you is saying you need to burn that stuff, all your drugs, your bad music, and your porn stuff. That is the way the Maker is working through your life right now. This is it. You have to make it right with your Lord Jesus. Now say. We need to stop playing around and get on the ball. We are jumping in and out of that path that God has for us. You know his plan, the future. We are passionate people going back to the basics. We are born to win. No matter what, he will come for you. Choose those things, which are up above. We have the spiritual DNA running through our veins. Jesus wants us to have full conversations with him. It is like we are talking to our family like husband and wife, like brother are sister. If you want to know and have an understanding of the power over the devil. Receive the Holy Spirit? I myself am full of his spirit. He put things in life that I can't do alone. Can you hear me, Jesus? I am calling out to you. Believe it or not, he is listening. He is closer than you think. Just remember this. Your hobbies that you do every day or once a week will become your greatest gifts for the world to see. I am talking about people. People can see it, smell it, touch it, and the most important thing is they can hear it, and all this comes from God, the Creator. All things are simple for him, but they are a big deal to us. So lean and learn the combination and formula of understanding about yourself. You can find yourself in him. Sometimes, you feel life gives you a curveball at that same time he is making you in his image. You can find the way back home to where you belong, your first love from the beginning. Somehow, someway you have been led astray. The world has been telling you that you are better than those so-called Christian folks who are weak in actions. OK, keep saying to yourself but there is something about you that people cannot understand. You are not your own self.

It is time for a wake-up call. It is time to go deeper in the Lord, so lock load because the enemy wants your soul to be tied down if he can wear out the soul he gets you where he wants you, so you question yourself, and you start to bend the Bible law's customizes it to your own way of thinking destroying and twisting the ten commitments. I do not know about this" one that they call those kind of people, Christian terrorist extremes get a life you feeble—minded people here. Do we need to call a time-out for you? Yes, I said it for you to exempt God out of your life. The consequence by changing is this: You think you can change God's plan for you or for your family. You tell me you have a decision to make. Be poor for the rest of your life, or keep on doing what you want to do, not letting go of your fears. Your future is calling you to the real you. And it is saying that is the way people in general look at you as if you are a funny, unknown person from another planet. You got to understand you are not your own when you hear his voice. He is the one who tells you what to do, where to go, what to say to this person when you see him and her the next time.

It is a divided purpose. Some how you have away of locking up the gift inside yourself until it becomes a big green fungus, and it keeps on growing until it overtakes you, your emotions keeps your mouth shut so what are you going to do about it the commits of a stupid devil always using his commentary words against you trying to do your best for god. On the side note proverbs 16:1-3 grab this:

1. The preparations of the heart in man, and the answer of the tongue is from the lord.
2. All the ways of a man are clean in his own eyes; but the lord weigheth the spirits.
3. Commit thy works unto the lord, and thy thoughts shall be established.

Grab this hold on to it and heaven for yourself we all need it, watch out for our salvation if you are really concern about it. For those people who like to work all the time and don't even have time to go to church, you are killing yourself for an early grave, acting like a scrooge toward your very own family. So get over it. This is the real truth of the matter. Do you even see it coming when you least expect it. So why me at this time? Right now, you do know how it feels to see your dad and mom crying. It hurts me to see them cry for something that is happening very bad, so I take all that inside me and try to use it for good.

That's why I am writing this book, to deal with real-life episodes series of events that you just can't deal with. Here is a walk through my life. You can judge from your point of view if you haven't already done so. You must go to God and let him direct your memory and your emotions to the place of your great heart wound (though you may very well have multiple deep heart wounds, there is probably one that God wants to focus on today). Ask God to show you where and how your heart has been damaged by the spiritual and emotional violence of living in a sinful world. Be willing to work with Jesus through any memory or emotion he brings up lingeringly. Don't be in a hurry. Let him hold you and share your tears. Ask God to show you if you have made a vow that you did not follow though ask for forgiveness to be renounced. When we fall, he picks us up to get back on that road for which we are traveling on right now. Oh, please God, set things in my life back together again. It has been done in the spiritual world. We have to do it ourselves. With God's help, we can make it.

Jesus, I renounce every vow I made. I made them to seal off my wound and protect myself from further pain. Reveal to me what those vows were. I break every agreement I have made with lies that came with my wounds. These are lies from Satan. I make all agreement with you, Jesus. I give the protection of my heart and soul back to you. I trust you with all that is within me. Father, who am I to you? You are my true Father, my Creator, my Redeemer, and my Sustainer. You know the man you had in mind when you made me. I do not want to play any more games with you anymore. I want you to speak to me, tell me what you think of me as a man. I also ask you to tell me any name you have for me. By doing this my true strength revealed what you specifically created me for, open my eyes that I might see give me ears to hear your voice. Father, I ask that you speak these things again and again, so that I might really receive it. Now grant me the courage to receive it now believe what you say and the faith to believe that it will come to pass in my life.

And they say that patience is a virtue. Back in my past, I was fighting the elements of the outside. Now that I am older, I am fighting with my flesh my inside self. My personal life has been affected. In this world, not being with other Christians as your self, we hear it all the time. Why are you so health conscious? Will your people consciously step out on faith and do this? I have this kind of problem with myself. I know this. It takes a long time to get over it; for some, it can be a quickie. That means cold turkey. I want to get to know me and I want the world to notice that we are facing with this being a better human dealing with stuff on a day to day basis, until we get to those white garments and changed into our new bodies no need to worry about a thing because you are home, free. Truly, we are facing dark times ahead. Lift your heads to the sky as the kingdom of heaven is near. More people are going to lose a lot of sleep. The voice of God will be at work real hard. Some people are in high-profile jobs, making bad decisions and do not know what's going on behind the scenes. Please do not get sucked into these worldly views. You have got to get smarter than that. Use your own logic.

And if you go to any pawnshop, just look around. You can see different lifestyle stuff that comes from everywhere. You can think people have ended their lives. Some began anew with the money they got, for they worked hard. You gave it up to perfect strangers. This was your last resort, and thinking twice about it proves to you that you can live without it now. Why are we doing this to Jesus, putting him on the sidelines? You do not have to think twice. He knows that you can't hold on. Keep your eyes on him. He will show you the way out. I am a true Christian; get me out. You have to just dust off your clothes. You have cleared the crust off your eyes. The problems in life will train you to get closer to Jesus. Please, people, do not be the one to gain the whole world and lose their own soul. I'm talking to my Lord by myself. Spending more time with your self is a good thing to do, to purify the soul of all that is not of God. From you to your god your wife or your kids and for all those single people out there you are not alone he is still working on you and you are going to know your purpose on this earth, why did he make me, he must knew what kind of mess I would be getting into the other way around.

Am I an artful kind of person? We all are different. Somehow, someway, we can change everything all around us, but we cannot take the time to change our very souls. You have to be right with God no matter what happens. Through all the four seasons, keep your soul pure and holy, for this is good for you and your loved ones who live with you day after day. Be the living example for your Lord Jesus who made the way for all of us. Don't quit. You have come a long way. Who cares what people think, when they see someone going the wrong way? "Shout out," to them, you are going the wrong way, and if they ask you, the people on the side lines say why if any at all, because I have been through that road before. I have experienced nothing but heartaches and a lot of addictions down that way. It is the story of my life. It is because God has changed me and blessed me in ways I did not know. I came clean and faced my fears head-on. You have to do it to, break the bondages over your life. Quit feeding the flesh, your sins. It will get you deeper and deeper in that hole you keep digging, and you will not be able to get out of it. Let me show you something here, your very own fifth sense. You can taste sin; you can smell sin. You can see sin. You can hear sin, and you can even touch sin. That is the basis, and the devil uses all that to gain some of his territory.

So what are you going to do about it? Will you be running away with your white flag at hand, saying, "I give up? I give you my soul to keep devil. You got to be kidding me." oh I don't think so this time devil, you keep on putting on the same trick with me year after year, and in the same month, and time this is what the devil do, in hell, he keeps on doing things to you over and over again well this time I'm having closer encounters of the God kind so eat that. Each morning when you get in the car, do you say a little prayer, trying to get your day started on the right track? You might be warming up your car or singing that song you heard in that Sunday church service. You must have the time to pray. Do not take life for granted. You are very important to God. You are his treasure. You may not feel like praying right now, you will. Just start praying, the words will come. It is OK to throw out something from your heart. Ask the Lord to help you, say Jesus I need help, in your kind of style, so do whatever works for you.

Tell him how you are feeling in your soul, in body. Don't think with your mind. Think with your soul. Tell the story. Go to your room. It does feel like a spiritual crime scene the day you got deeper in the Lord, deeper the spiritual fight begin Jesus changes things for you to get wiser, no more sleeping for you it is more watching and praying, so what is your map scope of life headed for, or you living it or missing it, life has passed you by. So come back to yourself, home is where the heart is, so go do that something you never did before. Know that people are dying every day, and any time of the day. And in that day, tomorrow is not promised. If you are a Christian, if not, come to your full purpose in your life be a Christian, take on the spiritual, a life without getting all provoked, and tested, the kind of person you need to become now, don't quit, stop worrying, you are not along struggling with your personal sin, trying to fit in, but you feel funny just doing that, feeling alone, and how long has it been sense your childhood came back up in that down turn, in that moment that the devil stole your childhood.

In this part of life, some people start early, and some people may start really late in life. Learning to get rid of it, and say to yourself, "Thank you, Jesus, for coming and completing this section of my life." So get it to together. You can make it and your whole family. God knows you more than you know your own self. You need to talk to someone close to you about this problem that you have. Do not keep it inside. When you do that, it starts to eat away your peace of mind, your eating habits will change, and the number one of all, getting no sleep for weeks or months or years you and your body will give up, so you are a work in progress," as a dirty jar for now. So what are you going to do I say this for a example. There are many types of glass jars, big ones, medium size, and small ones. You can fill them with all types of things, but the number one thing to put in those jars was coins, sense I was a little boy it was all about the money coins, which one are you the clean jar with no spots are the dirty jar, you cannot see through because of the brown coins. I call it your dark sins, and the silver coin I call, your white lies, sins, the ones we hide under the table and make them pretty in the light.

Are you fading away? Your face shows it. Your eyes used to be white and filled with life, and now they are dark and dim. Take one day at a time. Every hour and every minute, and every second counts. You are the soldier with sacred hands from battle. It shows up in your emotions, how to handle all kinds of different things the real deal about the spiritual world, to withstand the fiery darts of the devil, on his own turf. And being alone makes you stronger than ever. Why do we go through clashes of life like this? Do you really understand that you are better than this? So the holdup here is that you are a little slow in some things, but you are learning in time. So get your hands dirty for a change, get past self right now you are fighting for today your heart and soul, desire of your gifts that God has given you, ready to chase after it just to get close to your dreams remembering the glass jar, so run with it. Don't be scared. Jesus Christ gave it up. So you don't give up on your hidden talent. It will help hundreds of or even thousands of people, maybe just one. You did it. Give the glory to God, so let your light so shine before men, what is your last resort? It is the glass jar, myth full of money and vanity, are you going to hit the knees in your secret place, just you and your God.

Aren't there some times so strange that you cannot sleep, eat, or talk to anyone? You are so focused on the tasks at hand. I got to talk to someone out there who understands me. This is just to say there are a lot of people out there fighting with their real selves. Not trusting in your self, what decisions will affect you for life, or will I benefit for the right choice I made? And the choice is this: Should I keep on doing sin that is hurting my very soul? I keep on running in circles with the devil year after year. The painful thing it seems when, I really think over it, and that it keeps on creeping up. We cannot serve two masters a slave to one or the other a blessing of life. l am marked by the Maker's hand in order to mold me in his likeness so that my soul is rich. Now list the five things this year that you have learned. Has it been an easy year, or has it been a very hard year for you? And that list you have has grown ten to twenty times more, so I hope my list will help you out to remind you on some things that you had forgotten.

Learning more about the wonders of the meaning of things that people wouldn't even think of, more wisdom, being more open mindless, no more blind to the truths that God has for you, how to trust God with my problems like when money is tight right now but god will provide somehow or some way I give it to you Lord, I say it. And just keep on trusting in him to grow in that step by step process of life itself. Never stop learning about your God. No more lazy praying. Do you think that kind of praying reaches heaven? You know better than that. Do you ask yourself, "Why do I have to go through this prison of a life? I was not made for this. I really feel like Indiana Jones going through a trap room one after another, the road to my future. I cannot do this all by myself, so help Jesus. You lead me on."

For a while, I had been shaken up by the devil, but I'm hot as a real Christian should be. So I picked up my sword. That means your Bible and my shield to protect myself from the fiery darts, and did some devil killing. In doing so, I know you're going to have some mixed emotions now or later. I am not going to make up your mind for you but something like that. We need to help each other to find our strengths. We need to guard our soul. Why do you have echoes of the mind? You know that. So call the inner voice inside. How do I wonder about that thing you do? There is something wrong. You can feel it. When you do something right, you feel it. It's not so bad feeling that way so get a grip on yourself and feed on Jesus vibes not your own vibes your flesh will trick you about your own money and future. Do not have brief moments with the devil, say to the devil no more deals. No inside deals now we can make up for lost time, make up deals that are about you, can't make up your own mind God gave you. You see things are going to make sense to you like connecting the dots with lights on it.

I am in the devil-killing business. So are you with the devil, or are you not? It is your choice. As a heightened awareness kind of a person, you double think stuff and rehearse them and act them out. You find yourself profiling people wherever you go, out in a crowded place, tailgating, engaging in activities, irrespective of whether they are dangerous or not. We need to renounce the lie. Say it to yourself, "Teach me your ways, oh Lord Jesus, make me understand that I have freedom in God to rule and rein with him in heaven and earth." I want to make it to heaven and not be like the other people all boxed up killing each other here on the five o'clock news. Do not fall into a prison of yourself. You will go crazy, ready for the mental hospital. You need to fall into his merciful wings of glory, in the sweet presence of the Holy Spirit. While lying in bed, I start to look up at my ceiling, staring at it for a while, getting so comfortable, thinking about the events of the day. Can we understand, or can we reconcile ourselves in the bed that we lie in day after day? Problems of life seem to go away for a while. Just sitting there in our own, gathering thoughts, not understanding why it seems so complex for you in that you come to yourself that it is in God's hands. Let it go.

Have you ever sat at the mall, I mean really just sat there, and start to look around at the people, the many different lives that pass you by from all walks of life, of all colors, races, and the groups of families? And you can hear people laughing, children playing, babies crying. You see in a slow motion state that people are shopping, couples together are holding hands, the old folks are walking together with a rhythm. You see one old man walking slowly with his brown cane with him. You hear the real sound of life's noise by just listening to it. You will lose track of time or your sense of direction. Do not focus on the world to see it in that way, for you are walking with God at that moment. You hear lawyers say some times you can take that to the bank when their reaction there climax on their opening argument no arguments here when we all are climaxing to heaven, now use what you got from Jesus take it to others that are missing the hit of the Holy Spirit, that love that you once had for god long time ago well it is time to make a comeback not holding back take it to the cross please do not hide the cross leave open for all can see. Isaiah 59:1-2 Says.1 Behold, the Lord's hand is not shortened, that it cannot save; neither his ear heavy, that it cannot hear: 2. But your iniquities have separated between you and your God, and your sins have hid his face from you, that he will not hear. It will be helpful to read the Bible everyday of your life for your soul depends on it, it's good to feed the soul man.

Do you know why people are so messed up? We know it is the devil feeding them bad information, lies after lies. The one thing that happen to us we keep it inside our brains in a back file and over time we develop a certain habit to cover it up and when something major happen it triggers that thing I do not think the greatest movie makers can not copy the mind. Today it has not been cracked; the undiscovered human mind. You got to know this. In Romans 12:2-3 says. 1. And be not conformed to this world: but be ye transformed by the renewing of your mind, that ye may prove what is that good, and acceptable, and perfect, will of god. 3. For I say, through the grace given unto me, to every man that is among you, not to think of himself more highly than he ought to think; but to think soberly, according as God hath dealt to every man the measure of faith. Only the soul can rise up out of the fleshly body, and those things that happened to you years ago, or maybe when you were a child with that which, we tend to forget, but we don't. It is hidden away in the back of your mind, so we play it off for the rest of our lives, not knowing that with one push of that button and a ball that has been thrown in your program, it comes back in your darkest of dreams, out of nowhere. So the roller coaster begins, and the true person comes out the reason I say that because you have been faking it all this time tired between two worlds. John 16:33 says. These things I have spoken unto you, that in me ye might have peace.

In the world ye shall have tribulation: but be of good cheer; I have overcome the world.

Do you notice the things throughout your life? The stuff you stayed away from the good things of life, and I am talking about your first times. When that happens, your true colors are shining through. You are living life at the fullest, and don't tell me you have been through rush hour traffic for hours before and after work. What are you thinking about all those hours? I'd rather be some where else than here, god is not pushing you to do anything that will harm your very soul, and he sees everything that you are going throw. So hang onto your life saver ring to be full of Gods anointing in his or hers heart's desire to share to preach the real gospel to all the world you got to know that god is not races he is the one who made us in his image. Luke 4:18-19. Jesus says this. 18. The spirit of the lord is upon me, because he hath anointed me to preach the gospel to the poor; he hath sent me to heal the brokenhearted, to preach deliverance to the captives, and recovering of sight to the blind, to set at liberty them that are bruised. 19. To preach the acceptable year of the lord. But why people want to kill themselves whatever the problem great or small to go extremes for example buying a gun getting drugs off the street like cocaine for one and prescription drugs just trying to say to you. That you have a drinking problem and you can't sleep at night because of fighting with your own demons and overdosing is not the answer people. James 4:6-8 says this. 6. But he giveth more grace. Wherefore he saith, God resisteth the proud, but giveth grace unto the humble. 7. Submit yourselves therefore to god. Resist the devil, and he will flee from you. 8. Draw nigh to God, and he will draw nigh to you. Cleanse your hands, ye sinners; and purify your hearts, ye double minded.

I am telling you I have seen this throughout my lifetime. In the truth of the matter, it is not in our nature to kill ourselves I say no to that. Maybe it seems like that sometimes; you do understand all about God's promises? In saying, you never stop growing in god that the innocent year's were stolen from you at a early age wondering in time what's on the other side of this and another is strait function to deal with things as they pursed them. And to all the haters out there of prolife choices you hate life giving to this life to breathe the air into their lungs and for the race haters out there, you hate all other races but your own, you know who you are, we keep on saying this for years, look like some of us don't get the picture, in some things yes, but I've done this once before or said something to someone once before and in turn you cannot change the person only god can.

And God does not hate anyone, we hate. In this old sinful body, we have to share a common goal. To reach the higher calling of God's will, to be the best In God, we trust our very souls. Every single person is living and breathing on this planet, all 6.1 billon and more. Counting the bad, the good, and the ugly, the attitude of God in his infinite wisdom, he made us all out of the same dirt that you are standing on right now. Case is closed. Do you know what you can do with all that hate that has been building up inside of you for so long? All you need is to take it to the cross at the foot of Jesus. I mean you can touch the blood and water flowing at the foot of the cross. Jesus burn every hate known to mankind that was done to him. When they crucified him, he was dragging that cross down that long road of death. There were a lot of people in the crowd who had mixed emotions. Some were people who loved Jesus, and some others who hated, despised him and for what he stood for. There are a lot of people burning the cross to this day, so what are we going to do about that, you have to be before the people you have to look beyond their false and tell them keep your eyes on Jesus. All the learning starts when we were kids. With our young fresh minds, the devil could gain easy access. In kids minds like a computer virus 98 percent up rooted before the age of 9 more pressure in to submission to grab a hold of their minds. In that child's: body, that's why we have to train up a child teach them about God that is the right thing to do. In another case to hear some of the horrible stores to tell of a man that never grew up until the day he got released of his demands. I wonder which road he was traveling on, oh the worst case scenario road. 1 Corinthians 13:11. 11. When I was a child, I spake as a child, I understood as a child, I thought as a child: but when I became a man, I put away childish things.

Nobody wants to face their very own dark side you can see it in road rage. Most of the time people can flip the script like that, really quickly. On the highways of the twenty-first century with more people with more education than ever in their minds, but still there is the stupidest person on the wild America streets. I hate saying that can you bear with me with some of the truths. Can you feel the pain of childhood in America? But I might be turning a page to fast here. You have to give it to me. I am telling some of the truth; you can take it or leave it, to see the real true self, all 100 percent of you. I did not want to do the sinful life, and sinful quickies can last for ten to twenty years. You need to get a grip over your thoughts in life. Your mind is like a damaged product. Stop looking down on your self. It will destroy the closest person that you hold dear to you, so let it go. Holding on to the inner hate, is self-destruction. You can control it; mind control is just like a chase game. In that game that you have, you cannot show proof of purchase because it went in default in your very hands. Your dreams, your zeal for life are in there, but you can't touch them. Water of life winds of change in the high place to smell the winds of change in life to see things in a different way, the test we all been tested, and have showed the way so many times in our own life in the end, all the tools ever needed is from god to show the only way, all we really need is the grace that comes from god. Stop letting your mind go back, give your weary's to the lord. 2 Corinthians 10:3-6 this is very important. 3. For though we walk in the flesh, we do not war after the flesh: 4. (For the weapons of our warfare are not carnal, but mighty through god to the pulling down of strong holds;) 5. Casting down imaginations, and every high thing that exalteth itself against the knowledge of god, and bringing into captivity every thought to the obedience of Christ; 6. And having in a readinessto revenge all disobedience, when your obedience is fulfilled.

You got to feel and hold him in your arms. I have been a true believer here since the past twenty-two years. He has changed me so many times over, and that is OK with me right now. I gain so much knowledge now than three years ago. At this point, I had to make a decision to stay where I am or to change things forever. The more we pick and choose a lot in life as a unpredictable people, the more we can get ahead in this picking and choosing, do you have unreasonable fears that keeps on coming, it doesn't stop building up through time inside of you and still this is one of the biggest trials that is facing a growing Christian today. These recurring memories of my past hurts me. Yes, it happens sometime memories come back. That's why I am writing in this book. Quit living a double standard life. You do it sometimes. You do it when it is needed just to get through the day of working, You go to the movies, taking a lot of painkillers, or sometimes you just fall down, and know it is not you today you failed. You have to wake up out of a sleep estate, say it to yourself. I have a chance. It may make my soul free, for I know that, the son Jesus Christ is still shining on me from heaven. Showing love day by day. Love the people no matter what; one of the gifts from God is to bring forth your fruits.

Show me your ways, Lord. I want to understand your ways. I want to go all the way with you. No more short cuts all of my soul and all my heart belongs to you we choose how we want to be molded in the right way are wrong way of the world point of view, God himself can do this for you to show you the right way, so quit fighting it, I know it can be very painful, just go through it, he will do a good work in you. I ask myself, "Can I really love someone at this point in my life?" I do not know right now. So when I get there, I will let you know. It has been a lot of hit and miss. It has been a long time for me, so I am living the single life, for right now I know one of these days, it is coming for me, and I hope she's the one for me. Do you worry, sometimes, of the unknown fear? Do you worry about stuff that you are not supposed to worry about? Things should be in order but is not for you. In your mind, in your eyes, in your body, do you feel like organizing? Do you really know yourself, or your soul needs a special kind of inventory check. Do you need some spring-cleaning in your life and for your soul man inside? Jesus is the Mr. Clean. He will clean it up by the blood of Jesus Christ.

Have you ever tried to cry and you tried your best to bypass all the guilt and hurt from the past? or past relationships that failed you your best friend that turned their back from you, and all those years you been fighting for others, and know the gun barrel has somehow pointed back at you, that is call a blast from the past and now find yourself not making tears anymore. You feel cold as ice like a TV dinner, you or not hot for Christ like you use to be. And now you are cold for the devil serving him in his cold and dark places running away from promises that god had stored up for you and not having freedom within yourself you have to face it, tie up your belt buckle, because it is going to be a rocky ride baby, in so many ways, God is lending you back to him. I felt the freedom to hope, and dream like a child, going outside in my backyard when I was a little boy creating things out of the freedom doing what God wanted me to do so I did a lot of that back there and one of them was getting a regular egg from the refrigerator and taking it outside and putting it on the ground right beside that big tree. With a big pall of leafs right beside it and putting the egg inside the leafs right beside that big tree and cover it up with those leafs and stand there for a while, thinking that the egg will open up with a little baby chicken that would out, but after awhile I got teary eyed and ran inside my house with sadness thinking that everything would be all right. In this I wanted to see a miracle happen in front of my eyes maybe I wanted to see and believe there was a God up there, right now are you a repeat offender against God, for your sins that has been taking over your life.

Isaiah 59:1-21

1 Behold, the lord's hand is not shortened, that it cannot save; neither his ear heavy, that it cannot hear:

2But your iniquities have separated between you and your God, and your sins have hid his face from you, that he will not hear.

3 For your hands are defiled with blood, and your fingers with iniquity; your lips have spoken lies, your tongue hath muttered perverseness.

4None calleth for justice, nor any pleadeth for truth: they trust in vanity, and speak lies; they conceive mischief, and bring forth iniquity.

5They hatch cockatrice' eggs, and weave the spider's web: he that eateth of their eggs dieth, and that which is crushed breaketh out into a viper.

6Their webs shall not become garments, neither shall they cover themselves with their works: their works are works of iniquity, and the act of violence is in their hands.

7Their feet run to evil, and they make haste to shed innocent blood: their thoughts are thoughts of iniquity; wasting and destruction are in their paths.

8The way of peace they know not; and there is no judgment in their goings: they have made them crooked paths: whosoever goeth therein shall not know peace.

9Therefore is judgment far from us, neither doth justice overtake us: we wait for light, but behold obscurity; for brightness, but we walk in darkness.

10We grope for the wall like the blind, and we grope as if we had no eyes: we stumble at noonday as in the night; we are in desolate places as dead men.

11We roar all like bears, and mourn sore like doves: we look for judgment, but there is none; for salvation, but it is far off from us.

12For our transgressions are multiplied before thee, and our sins testify against us: for our transgressions are with us; and as for our iniquities, we know them.

13In transgressing and lying against the LORD, and departing away from our GOD, speaking oppression and revolt, conceiving and uttering from the heart words of falsehood.

14And judgment is turned away backward, and justice standeth afar off: for truth is fallen in the street, and equity cannot enter.

15Yea, truth faileth; and he that departeth from evil maketh himself a prey: and the LORD saw it, and it displeased him that there was no judgment.

16And he saw that there was no man, and wondered that there was no intercessor: therefore his arm brought salvation unto him; and his righteousness, it sustained him.

17For he put on righteousness as a breastplate, and a helmet of salvation upon his head; and he put on the garments of vengeance for clothing, and was clad with zeal as a cloke.

18According to their deeds, accordingly he will repay, fury to his adversaries, recompence to his enemies; to the islands he will repay recompence.

19So shall they fear the nameof the LORD from the west, and his glory from the rising of the sun. When the enemy shall come in like a flood, the spirit of the LORD shall lift up a standard against him.

20And the Redeemer shall come to Zion, and unto them that turn from transgression in Jacob, saith the LORD.

21As for me, this is my covenant with them, saith the LORD; My spirit that is upon thee, and my words which I have put in thy mouth, shall not depart out of my mouth, nor out of the mouth of thy seed, nor out of the mouth of thy seed's seed, saith the LORD, from henceforth and forever.

*a*re you well aware of that fear? Yes, I am aware of my fear, but sometimes it overtakes me so badly that I keep it inside and we hide it so well some of us even beat the actors in Hollywood, at their on art, by putting on a act for them, it is fake and for us we have to live with it everyday for a long period of time, until something breaks your soul to yield to his Holy Spirit. A point of returning really choosing the God option not stock option because he does not go up and down with his emotions, and you don't trust in him do you, always me myself and I, so things with you make you proud and a stand up man or woman quit being so uptight with proudest and you don't want to talk to nobody you got to relax, just be yourself let God control the problems you are facing today this week or this month. Where is God calling you, out of hiding? At this point, he is still working on me. So I am going through this with his hope and grace, with the faith that I have inside of me to come out of one self. He is always calling us all out. We don't focus all the time; we just don't do it. The things you hope and pray for will never be called on, unless you take the lead. Why do you fear them? It has been a long time coming for some people's stuff, you thought it was over but they came back in your life and you gained straight along the way I thank God for teaching us, and molding us, and calling on him for direction to be lead on, to carry on the light that God gave you a long time ago, and now you're on the right road to talk to him, maybe later when I am ready for Gods comments. So you put it on hold for now. You see, that is why we don't get blessed by God. We are always quitting, always putting God on hold, for some people, they like to play with God. That's dangerous and does not give a chance for Jesus to talk to you, not at you. And now talk to him, saying, "What is the list that you want me to do in my life today, Lord?

I am desperate for him. I am running out of resources, running out of self-control. I can't sleep sometimes. I can't eat. If you can relate to me in this book, if you really seeing the big picture of what is going on walking through life on neutral. For every bad thing that has happened to you, that thing you say all the time, it just comes right out. Why me, God? He is trying to help you. Who will stand in the services to find themselves, to lose yourselves in the moment? Relax, take one day at a time. You look like your own enemy who is trying to mold and shape you into this world, that very enemy who we are fighting against. And most of all he is very sneaky in every possible move that you make, always one step ahead of your game. After awhile you are being that person you did not want to be, and now it is too late in the game and too late to go back, and now you are walking, talking, thinking the next fix the hand adjusters knowing you are the professional actor of life the poker face liar and sometimes a back stabber.

Who's controlling who, and who has the remote control, you or the devil? And another thing is you feel sometimes that you're on the last string, at the last survival skills. It is a long time coming all by yourself. It is like that secret agent Jason Bourne. I am a Christian. I see movies too, and right now we are living it, the last food, the last medicine, last gas for your car, last wisdom, your last job on planet earth. There is not enough to go around, you say, but the one thing will not go away. You must use your last choice; that is to hang onto Jesus Christ. He will not let you down no matter what the problem is. You do not know what the future holds, so I am living day by day.1 Peter 5:6-9 is very important to know that. 6. Humble yourselves therefore under the mighty hand of God, that he may exalt you in due time: 7. Casting all your care upon him;

for he careth for you. 8. Be sober, be vigilant; because your adversary the devil, comes as a roaring lion, walketh about, seeking whom he may devour: 9. Whom resist stedfast in the faith, knowing that the same afflictions are accomplished in your brethren that are in the world. The day that you have to tell them your secret sins, which you are carrying with you, shutting out your family from your life completely, that's wrong to do. We must stick together for the long haul, as you call it the unity. Is Life itself getting harder for you right now, or you got it all, a carefree life, no bills to pay. Everything you got is paid for, your house, cars, and your bank accounts full of money, so what's next for you now?

So many things running through our minds that's so crazy, losing it and getting out of control we have human errors running through our DNA and blood. This is what the devil does he wants to kill you, drug you and drink ourselves away. We stop caring about the things that meant a lot to us. The things we always think about, the past, and how it brings up anger that we not suppose to have against our parents our brothers and sisters step dad or step mom, knowing how to deal with the cards that has been handed out to you. You are still a little kid in a lot of ways. Something is missing from your life. You keep it in the back of your mind, and at times you debate to yourself, trying to bet yourself, and you become a damaged good, a misfit of life who can't keep a job. You are always broke; your bank account is overdrawn, and the spirit man in you has been on an very Low Low profile life so what's going on with that. Proverbs 28:11-14 says this. 11. The rich man is wise in his own conceit; but the poor that hath understanding searcheth him out. 12. When rightous men do rejoice, there is great glory: but when the wicked rise, a man is hidden. 13. He that covereth his sins shall not prosper: but whoso confesseth and forsaketh them shall have mercy. 14. Happy is the man that feareth alway: but he that hardeneth his heart shall fall into mischief.

How can we change ourselves in the time zone we are living in? It sometimes seems like you have been here before and don't realize it until you know this at that exact moment it happened in your face, For once in my life, I like to get the devil before I sin. To know that the choice you made can help me or damage me forever what to do Lord. I do not even know it myself. The reason I said that is because we are always feeling sorry for ourselves, thinking about our sins. As time goes by, it becomes a cancer eating away at you the real person your soul man is in jeopardy. We fall down to our knees in the act of desperation you scream out Jesus help me, if Jesus told you today you need to feel real again. Has he been telling you that lately during your worship time with God? We need to shift gears without the devil noticing. As I write this book at this time, it has been one of my passions. It has some moments. I did not have time for some people in my life. I just told them I got to do this. So I just can't put my finger on it right now I am in a learning process right now so I am trying to get it and making it click for me. Do you feel like you are the missing link of life places that you are not suppose to be feeling out of your element kind of style, you feel out of place and your future is calling you out, it feels good at that moment and then you get scared of it. And say to yourself I do not have the spirit of fear but a sound mind, you are not crazy you just don't know your direction in life so there goes another route that has passed you by, there goes the road blocks of your purpose in life. Isaiah 40:30-31 says this. 30. Even the youths shall faint and be weary, and the young men shall utterly fall: 31. But they that wait upon the Lord shall renew their strength; they shall mount up with wings as eagles; they shall run, and not be weary; and they shall walk, and not faint.

I am hearing accosts of his voices from heaven calling out to me. At this time, I know it is Jesus talking to me at 3:30 a.m. in the morning when I am sleeping in my bed after a long day at work. So I wake up on my stomach. I flop back on my back after a deep sleep of dreaming and then it happens. The voice of the Lord saying to me how to face the day, and for the days to come. This is why I am writing this kind of book for a purpose. This has never happened to me like this before. I do not know what God is trying to do with me right now, so this is one of them. What are you doing on this earth, for the Lord or for yourself? Are you making a difference in other people's lives, are you just keeping it to yourself, saving it for a rainy day, and you keep on telling yourself, "I try so hard, and at the end, it really doesn't matter in any more ways." So do you really know how big our god is he will blow your mind so grab a hold on your gifts from him he has created a good thing in you. Those kinds of people like to put their minds in a desolate place a very bleak frame of a place with no air squeezing the young life to hold on to you see it there it is reaching out to you with the life line guide to Jesus. You got to know "this", the devil wants' to kill you to destroy all of you, so he can destroy this body which is call flesh but he cannot destroy the soul that belongs to God if you give it to him, alone the devil does not have the say so, god does. I know life is killing you dealing with other people's problems, and you keep on taking it, I am not God you are not a superhero.

I am a real person with feelings. There are people with no feelings. The devil has been taking their minds, bodies, doing evil works. I say to you right now all evil things must come to an end. I am sick and tired of the rich getting richer and the poor getting poorer. Running over people is not the answer and the old saying go's were there is a question there is an answer so I am not jointing them I won't to beat them at there on game. We choose how we want to be, a misguided mold, a life with the devil, or with Gods out come depends on you, let him mold and shape you, "Jesus" is the way made easy, so quite fighting with yourself. Why do you keep on avoiding God? Like that, you choose not to hear from God, locking up your soul, stopping up your ears like a water tub stopper. You do not want to hear his voice in your life, so tell me how do you make it without Jesus Christ in your life today? His touch makes your spirit grow stronger. He came from heaven to earth to show us the way to him. So make it loud and clear, to him that you want him in your life. Be bold. Declare this message that Jesus is Lord over everything take him where every you go, to the bookstore, to the coffee shop, to the beauty salon, to the grocery store, to the car dealership, to the fast-food joint, to the gas station, to the library, to the sports events that goes on the weekends. We have to make a stand for Jesus. People are dying every day by the minutes.

OK, God I am hearing you now. you got me. I have tried everything you have backed me up in the closet my tears are falling. Can you understand yourself in the good emotions or bad emotions the self conflicting thing is do you understand the father God and his son Jesus, and the holy spirit that is call the trinity, as one working for you like your cell phone networking there is a whole lot of people working on you the customer. He does not satisfy your flesh he sanctifies your soul man your spirit that is the real deal, about Jesus you do not have to sign a contract, he did all the work at the cross so when you start to talk to him there is no hang ups no static. Do you really know what god is thinking right now, for one, you and me, are we going to make the right decision about ourselves what to make of yourself have you found your combination code of life have you found the final lock to open that door that you were trying to open.

Your passion your gift keeps you up at night can't let it go and after awhile you start to know and it clicks, I might be helping someone with a great gift from God. And they came with a great responsibility. So come on, oh ye of little faith and go through that door of peace, joy and happiness so lay all your cares upon Jesus right now just stop whatever you are doing and let it go. Bring life to a point, to a broken heart, to find freedom to know who you really are to fill a wholeness to bring it to the world who are dyeing everyday, and as the spirit guides us to his perfect will. We ask the Lord to help a person to find his or her way to discover him, and speak the truth into their very own hearts, the authority of Jesus, it is his job to release you from your demonic oppression influences which blocking a person's healing and full walk with god. I need to, keep my intimacy with Jesus fully alive we all need to talk to him on a regularly basis you got to remember Jesus loves you he feels your love for him he helps me every time I run to the cross when I need to at any given time.

Time right now is speeding up there is a lot of stuff going on in the world today one of them are, the signs of the times sayings the ozone layers of the earth's atmosphere is decaying big huge chunks of ice falling into the sea and melting at the same time, because the sun it seems like the sun is getting closer because the earth is getting unprotected, earth quarks big huge waves of water the gas prices and food prices are going up people are getting laid off from there twenty year old jobs, their whole life depending on their pensions which is gone also robbery, stealing and none sense killing, destroying property, the thieves of this time are very bold with no feelings for life.

But one thing, they do not know there is a bold presents of the "Lord" watching our every move and Christians who will not stand unjust acts, as well as our Lord, these days. We have more unawareness in Jesus, Christians are everywhere people are singing the praises of the lord, and now even more. We have to tell every one we see the good news. When we are shopping out and about at the gas station talking about Jesus that he solves your problems. Romans 1:15-17 read this. 15. So, as much as in me is, I am ready to preach the gospel to you that are at Rome also. 16. For I am not ashamed of the gospel of Christ: for it is the power of God unto salvation to every one that believeth; to the Jew first, and also to the Greek. 17. For therein is the righteousness of God revealed from faith to faith: as it is written, the just shall live by faith.

We can get caught up in the affairs of the world very easily without noticing. We get caught in fame, riches, cars, women, houses, drugs, sex, clothes, hairstyles, or in watching movies at home or at the movie theater, jumping into that role-playing act of playing that person in the movie. You do it so much that it controls your mind and body, feeding the flesh. And what it wants from you depends on how far you let your flesh take over. We do linger in our sins like pigs playing in the mud. Oh God help us all. It is time to stop cold turkey. "Yes, I said it. God brings things into our lives for a purpose. It comes up without you knowing it until the end. So do you have what it takes for God who so loved our souls? Just remember not the flesh. When you have been through a lot of stuff for a long period of time, songs that you used to sing, you don't sing them anymore. And now it starts to make sense to you. The world always has a four-road intersection with us; which way do I go? I am getting tired of this. What you got to do, is let God do it for you. Keep your peace of mind.

In references to this part, here are some Bible verses to follow by: Psalm 40:1-4 this one says. 1. I waited patiently for the lord; and he inclined unto me, and heard my cry. 2. He brought me up also out of an horrible pit, out of the miry clay, and set my feet upon a rock, and established my goings. 3. And he hath put a new song in my mouth, even praise unto our God: many shall see it, and fear, and shall trust in the Lord. 4. Blessed is that man that maketh the Lord his trust, and respecteth not the proud, nor such as turn aside to lies. Psalm 62:5-8 says. 5. My soul, wait thou only upon God; for my expectation is from him. 6. He only is my rock and my salvation: he is my defence; I shall not be moved. 7. In God is my salvation and my glory: the rock of my strength, and my refuge, is in God. 8. Trust in him at all times; ye people, pour out your heart before him: God is a refuge for us. Psalm 32:6-7, 6. For this shall every one that is godly pray unto thee in a time when thou mayest be found: surely in the floods of great waters they shall not come nigh unto him. 7. Thou art my hiding place; thou shalt preserve me from trouble; thou shalt compass me about with songs of deliverance. I choose to believe on Jesus through this life I am tired of being a failure I must be in his refuge run to him the peace is in the God that you are seeking, my hiding place is in the Lord I choose, I'm trying to make it for myself. All of us must be addicted to Jesus at all times. We want him to listen to our soul, and our prayers we must focus on him. We got to keep our eyes on Jesus even in the good times and bad times on the weekends too. He will be strong for you. I want you to follow Jesus in the Bible. So give yourself, and your soul breathing room.

I ask of you not to give up your right as a Christian believer and your faith. If you have a burning inside for him, you are traveling the right road. So let him talk to you by all means, let him refill, renew all of you. We all will be with him some day very soon. He wants us to claim victory in your closet and pray, Lord thy will be done in earth as it is in heaven touched my heart my soul my life, in your best defense he is there when you need him. Jesus has not given up on us. On the cross he died so we should give it up to him with passion. Our deep fears make us stronger more tougher more focus on the task at hand you could be the best person for the job and when that day come don't say why me Lord because you have been chosen from the day of your birth it is in you this is what you are trained for your whole life, so do it.

I try not to think or even dwell upon my own troubles. It is too depressing. I try to think that this day is the best day of my life. Live to the fullest. You're stronger than yesterday. Have a joyride with Jesus; it is the best trip you will ever have. Pick two days every week for one month. Make it a day of quiet time for yourself and with the Lord. Try not to think about this world. Clear your mind. Let it go, all that fear, hate, and mixed feelings, no kids, no bills.Just by yourself, go out and do your thing, the stuff that you have put off for years. Try not to just get by. Try to make it. Do things that you have not done before out of your element, out of your comfort zone like going to church, fake sleepless zone that you are in. Do you know or remember what the Bible says? It says Jesus is our high tower and that he watches over us by day and by night. He comes when we are in trouble, in times of need. He comes not only during troubles but all the time. Try continually praising his name, seeking his face, and while on your face and knees, try to keep your soul. Quit looking down on yourself, for you are the temple of the Holy Ghost. Now if your temple which is your body has not the Holy Ghost. Ask God for it, because the Holy Ghost or Holy Spirit some like to say are the same, and we need it, God sent the Holy Ghost as a conforter to us, and a guide, this is his spirit. It will help you not to sin that if you want to, God does not make you stop sinning he's has given us free will it's up to us.

Bring truth to your lives. God is telling you to do this. Walk and keep your eyes on Jesus, on your good and bad week. Maybe the stock market is taking a beating on you right now. Keeping your peace of mind and good health is important. Families are eating together at the dinner table in doing that relieves stress in the body, and some are not eating together. Coming back together is a symbol of unity. I can see now. I know that is the best thing God has given us, is the Holy Ghost that when you feel bad spirits of the enemy are coming to attack, the Holy Spirit let's you know, that's what God gave us to define ourselves from the devil. At that tough time. Today the devil comes in different shapes and forms, in darkness and in the light, even reading between the lines. He can trick you with the smallest words on the contract that you did not see it coming, you just skip that part all together. You do not know it relates to your problem, so today the devil used your boss and your work phone. That we use out in the field challenging me to the dull with Coney words sneaky in every way words behind words trying to get to me using Gods name in vain in all of this, it was like at that moment I have to say here wake up people the enemy is coming for you all kinds of ways you maybe feeling weak in your body from working a lot, not knowing what tomorrow brings keep the faith.

Some of my days have been long, and I have been so very busy during the nights that I am very tired. The devil fights me a lot yes, because he knows that I'm carrying the message of God, we all at one time or another will just blow it off sometimes. We do that with the answer machines putting things on hold. So you lie there in your bed, and you start to open your mouth, you have had battles fighting with the devil reminding him saying that Jesus Christ died on the cross, for your sins and you order the devil to leave in the name of Jesus. And then you close your eyes and go back to sleep. Minutes pass by. You can feel the room go clear. It feels real thick and heavy at first it is because of all the fighting going on in the spirit with the angels and demons on my behalf it does not fell so crowed as once before. Now it is just me and the Lord. That's all I ever needed from him, just a little push, and I will be on my way. People are always using magnifiers in their life, adding stuff, or trying to cover it up and not letting God monitor for them. We all, somehow or someway, have been affected by or have been arrested by the world. These are some of the common reflections we keep on putting the old stuff back on the shelf, not putting new ones.

Your job, your marriage, addiction to drugs, repetition of a constant sin battle and past family sins, always come up every year after year, and you are paying for it irrespective of whatever you are dealing with right now. Not only that, your spirally life has gone down the drain. These mixed emotions affect the way you are living right now. Do not play any more games. Believe me, if you keep yourself busy doing God's work, your sins will have no room in your life. In time, it will go away. Keep your mind and thoughts on him. Do not think of negative thoughts anymore. It will cause cancer in your life, if you let it. Short or long term, it is your choice. You are created in the image of God. Are the spots of life taking you over to the brink of non-existence? We cause pain for ourselves. Do you really believe that God can help you with your Christian walk? Don't give up. The day is not promised, but we thank God for the air we breathe. Thank you for one more day, Lord for the sun is shining through my window and through all of that, he will guide you to your right course. Yes you can have your mind set, but that is of the flesh, who knows what you have on your heart and soul, set it on God at all times, keep saying to yourself unbreakable soul nothing cannot change me I am gods property. If we keep it inside of us, you will grow out of those old bones you have been carrying. You are not broken. You have a strong body supported by Jesus, who will speak to you with compassion. Try to be as much like Jesus, humble yourself. In this look to Jesus he will see you through giving your cares over to god doing the right thing brings revival to yourself. Hebrews 12:1-3 look this up. 1. Wherefore seeing we also are compassed about with so great a cloud of witnesses, let us lay aside every weight, and the sin which doth so easily beset us, and let us run with patience the race that is set before us. 2. Looking unto Jesus the author and finisher of our faith; who for the joy that was set before him endured the cross, despising the shame, and is set down at the right hand of the throne of God. 3. For consider him that endured such contradiction of sinners against himself, lest ye be wearied and faint in your minds. Do you really want to win souls for Jesus? You got to be bold when you are at the gas station, pumping your gas. Say something about the day how the lord has blessed us just a little. They will get the message quickly. It always helps when someone needs help, they were thinking about problems they had from a distance. Try finding something to work with. When you are standing in line at the grocery store, say something like, "I love the Lord." You have the freedom of speech. Do what you got to do. Some people would won't to know how they can know about Jesus. I am trying to be real with this, the best I can. So please keep reading this. I know it will help you in the long run, in some form or fashion. We have millions of cars on the roads and people are dyeing everyday on that freeway in rush hour when the traffic moves fast or slow. They see on the back of a car Jesus Loves You, it makes them think why am I here is Jesus the one that made me in his image, he must love me a lot. We have a lot of things that we have no control over problems take over our emotions we get depressed we have nowhere to turn someone has been abused. So we keep on living with this for the rest of our lives until we reach our deathbed. This is too much for one person to handle. This is only the beginning of the downward spiral in your personal life. If the enemy which is the devil gets you to think that you are sick you will dwell on that. Once there were no more road trips for you it became the end of the road for you. Really you have too many choices in life for you to give up, so what is going to be your job here. So what is your story in this crazy world that we are living in? Don't get me wrong I love America, but some things have gone and lifted, in some bad things I almost want to say spiral politics. It is time for people to stand on top of the table shouting out, "I do believe in Jesus Christ." a true act of love toward the people now is time to turn on the light on some things. Because we are the next generation it's time to make a stand for what is right, and it is to teach our young people, to help them to step up to the plate love them guide them. I am sitting at a panic table on a mountain top, calling, praying over the mountain which is overlooking the city. And as I am sitting here in the woods, I close my eyes, I'm feeling really good and I hear the effects of the wind on the environment. I hear wood cracking. I see the tree limbs falling, trees swaying. I hear squirrels running across tree limbs, and as I am opening my eyes, I can see the squirrels jumping off them. I rather join the squirrels because I don't have to put on my survival skills; and here no pressure here not today it is all about having faith in yourself and talking to God. To really find yourself, go to the woods. It is the best sound system you would ever get at some far-off place like this, a place were you have never been before. Go to your secret place; it is like chicken soup for the soul. Let your soul be free. Give it time to download some peace from God. Let him rebuild, your road that is coming apart in that let him remold you so that the things you ever wanted will come to you, your dreams projects programs. Do some communitie service with the church, to feed homeless, little by little. He is changing me; I am no stone with a cold heart here. As a small child, you I wanted Mom and Dad when you were trying to go to bed. You wanted them when you were facing the darkness and fear itself. Most adults run away from their fears and problems. They let them control them, and that has been happening lately in your life. Things keep on showing up out of nowhere, without notice. So what if they fired you from your job or gave you a pink slip? And the last resort is, you want to leave God out of your life. You need him. So praise him because he will not leave you or forsake you ever. He will fix you up. He will blow your mind. Psalm 91:1-9 says. 1. He that dwelleth in the secret place of the most High shall abide under the shadow of the Almighty. 2. I will say of the Lord, he is my refuge and my fortress: my God; in him will I trust. 3. Surely he shall deliver thee from the snare of the fowler, and from the noisome pestilence. 4. He shall cover thee with his feathers, and under his wings shalt thou trust: his truth shall be thy shield and buckler. 5. Thou shalt not be afraid for the terror by night; nor for the arrow that flieth by day. 6. Nor for the pestilence that walketh in darkness; nor for the destruction that wasteth at noonday. 7. A thousand shall fall at thy side, and ten thousand at thy right hand; but it shall not come nigh thee. 8. Only with thine eyes shalt thou behold and see the reward of the wicked.

9. Because thou hast made the Lord, which is my refuge, even the most High, thy habitation; You just can't walk away like a secret agent. It is in you. I call it God's back-up plan. Choose the road, which is less traveled. We all know the answer. Sometimes, it is just in front of us. We just don't know it at the point of desperation when we are busy checking ourselves you think. Do I use my last lifeline, or do I keep on going to see, irrespective of wherever it leads me on to? God wants us to seek him when you have nothing else to turn to, when you done all you could, when it is your last meal, your last gas money, when all the money is gone went from your life. Then you wonder, what's next? We can be our own worse enemy. We cannot trust ourselves in some things. We keep drinking in that bottle of beer, or trusting in the lottery ticket. But how low can you get while thinking of survival and not even obeying the warning lights of the night? People really plan their weekends of sin very well, from the start to the finish. We can't even plan our own soul salvation. It is the truth. You think I have to say it again. "Quit" blaming God for your actions. I don't want to go back to the old self, again ever, to the evil thinking. So you want to be a tough attitude kind of a person. Go ahead with that for the rest of your life. See where it leads you maybe to the bottom of a pit. The Lord love's us. But he will not tolerate sin. Ezekiel 18:4-7. 4. Behold, all souls are mine; as the soul of the father, so also the soul of the son is mine: the soul that sinneth, it shall die. 5. But if a man be just, and do that which is lawful and right. 6. And hath not eaten upon the mountains, neither hath lifted up his eyes to the idols of the house of Israel, neither hath defiled his neighbour's wife, neither hath come near to a menstruous woman. 7. And hath not oppressed any, but hath restored to the debtor his pledge, hath spoiled none by violence, hath given his bread to the hungry, and hath covered the naked with a garment; Romans 12:1-2. 1. I beseech you therefore, brethren, by the mercies of God, that ye present your bodies a living sacrifice, holy, acceptable unto God, which is your reasonable service. 2. And be not conformed to this world; but be ye transformed by the renewing of your mind,

that ye may prove what is that good, and acceptable, and perfect, will of God.

Now It's time for a new fresh walk a changed soul, ready to win a soul for Jesus and not turning back to those things that you use to do, listen what ever you lost the Lord will give it back to you 100 times more, the Lord will bless the rights of those who serve him for your whole in tear life. Thinking of a Jesus plan, what's next, the undiscovered soul new thinking I have been reborn again a change in me the real me a free me it's a good thing ideal to give thanks to god everyday, to the giver of life. I want to keep on following up with you in Bible scriptures to gain more insight on things here so read these: Ephesians 2:2-5. 2. Wherein in time past ye walked according to the course of this world, according to the prince of the power of the air, the spirit that now worketh in the children of disobedience: 3. Among whom also we all had our conversation in times past in the lust of our flesh, and fulfilling the desires of the flesh and of the mind; and were by nature the children of wrath, even as others. 4. But God, who is rich in mercy, for his great love wherewith he loved us, 5. Even when we were dead in sins, hath quickened us together with Christ, (by grace ye are saved;) and this one. Colossians 2:6-8. 2. As ye have therefore received Christ Jesus the Lord, so walk ye in him: 7. Rooted and built up in him, and stablished in the faith, as ye have been taught, abounding therein with thanksgiving. 8. Beware lest any man spoil you through philosophy and vain deceit, after the tradition of men, after the rudiments of the world, and not after Christ. 9. For in him dwelleth all the fullness of the Godhead bodily. 10. And ye are complete in him, which is the head of all principality and power: We are not crazy to give up the things we love, but the one thing we must do is protect our souls from total domination and taking care of our love ones around us every single day making sure we teach our teenagers about Christ and putting up with sin in our lives like if we were flashing around like a banner the only thing I want in my life is the banner of Jesus in my heart to stay. Say to yourself so what kind of chains does the devil have you in that is call bondage, depression, sickness, and hatred. I am tired of worrying about things that you should not be worrying about. All this causes frustration of the mind and body, and the soul is in the middle of it, trying to do therapy to my own self it don't work. So I go to the Lord for help so I go and pray. This is the road less traveled, yes some of us do not like to pray, instead we worry about our bills our jobs and for some of you worry about your future wife or husband your car and your home. There is always a solution to a problem. It comes to an end. You got to remember to have faith in God he bought you this far. Get a grip on life as a human being. You think you are going crazy, but you are not. We need to quit flapping out when things go wrong. Some tests can be good for us some test come just to see how far your faith will take you, the lord knows how much you can bear. Somehow or someway, your spirit man has to be upgraded for the kind of level the lord wants' to take you. Is your attitude of life or your Christian life line up with Gods standers you must have some kind of disciple in order to function. What is the thing that makes you tick. What ever it is will come out and the test will make you stronger, you must feed the soul more vitamins meaning the bible, read it in your daily living no more quickies. You have been fighting for a long time, saying to yourself, "This battle is never going to end. I know it is impossible to fight by yourself. I know that I am not alone, battling for the Lord" Even now, you are losing brain cells. Are you losing soul cells right now, getting blindsided by the minute and by the day? So somehow you are going to protect yourself from all this sin. Just remember the devil. He cannot make you do bad things. No more in pulsing is he or is he not what kind of thinking is that. Jesus steps in when the time comes, it is up to you to make the choice and who is the author and the finisher of your faith Jesus is. Putting on a part time love and not a full time love does not work, did Jesus give part time love on the cross, you have to go all the way, you say you have love, doing all kinds of things, slow down, there are too many things happening in this world. We can count on the times we shared our love with other people to see the true Christ through us. Jesus does not see you in a wheelchair. He sees you walking. And well and understanding that kind of peace that passes all understanding. There is only one true voice. It is the Bible, the words of Jesus that speaks to your soul. Do you hate it when you are trying to serve God with all your heart and the devil knows it? He is just saying to himself, "I am really going to test this so-called real Christian, and he is really throwing some stuff at you." Little at a time, you should be throwing back Bible verses left and right at him. But the devil thought you could not remember your Bible verses, just like that I got where I can rebuke the devil and said it is in my heart and soul forever, oh here comes some peace that you order from god the happy hour special.

A true measure of a man Jesus Christ him self is when he has been tested how far he can go without backing down on a fight for the cross to the grave from the grave to the sky now that's a fight. Have the mind of Christ dead set on your goal, time is running out for the people God has appointed some people to do his work, for some of those people they are a little too slow, time to pick up the pace how long it's going to take has it been ten or twenty years it is time to graduate to a higher level don't you think. Some things in life will make you humble yourself. Just remember your time will come, and you will shine through the whole thing. You will know what to do at the right time and at the right place. It is all yours for the taking. People choose their own fate. Their own actions will determine how they will grow old gracefully. You have to hold wisdom in your hands and let it go. When you were young, you did not know your purpose in life, then, you Always thought positively about everything you do in life, at home, at work, with your family. Try not to think bad thoughts that are of the devil. Shut your ears, and open up your soul. As you move to God's way, the world's way comes to beat you down to the ground. It is true that as we move away from the light of Jesus way, the worldly things that you once loved will strangely go dim and find your way into an ever-lasting darkness. To do something for Jesus, you must do it totally. Your soul must be clean in order to go after something that you believe in. That time is speeding up and the end is coming soon. We must all work together. We must preserve our soul man for the greater cause and spread the word of Jesus. The time has come. Stop playing around and stop saying to yourself, "I have plenty of time." Repent of your sins now. Turn away from your wicked ways and there is a lot of people out there that do know there is a HELL there will be false prophet's claiming there way is the only way. Do not let the devil destroy your foundation. It took you a very long time to build it. Stay strong in the Lord. If I told you in this book already the very thing that the devil want's to do is separate families cause you to lose your homes, cars, jobs, and bank accounts, there 401K, s the pension plan you had planned is gone. And who are we going to trust in now, I know that the future is gone for you saying to yourself, where is the hope I once knew. And hope does not disappoint us, because God has poured out his love into our hearts by the holy spirit, whom he has given us.

I am here still alive, the devil has not killed me off in the scene, so what's up. I am still standing here, my deliver is talking to me saying I will lead you on I will give you peace keep saying to yourself I won't my dreams to come to pass this is not the end for me, this is only the beginning I am a solider in the army of the lord. Jesus you are really doing something in my life things all around me are changing, and charging me so keep on doing the work of the lord, you are really doing something this had to happen in order for the next big thing to come forth. Speaking of coming forth, it has been raining all day, and it is still cloudy and some parts of the sun try to come out. You are seeing this from a far off place, standing on that hill. You can see so clear the beams of light are going through the cracks of the clouds in the sky. When the sun shines through those beams, it makes me wonder when the rapture takes place, and all of Gods saints are shooting up through those clouds from the earth to the sky this is were the Lord comes back to take the Christians to heaven. Lord, I lift my eyes and my hands to you saying, "Jesus, I made it." Can you see it now? I know, can you feel it too. When a soul asks Jesus Christ to come into their heart, when they make that choice saying yes lord, then that very light from heaven shines on them the real truth comes in. And for that new believer, that is the way they can see things more clearly, the anointing is over shadowing them, they can feel him and when their eyes come open they see things more clearly than ever before. I say Lord you lift me up in the morning, and you keep me up at night, watching and praying. Lord, I thank you for watching over me. Without that, I could have been dead by now, and I hope you are saying the same prayer or something like that, your dreams have not turned to dust, so get up and go get them. Move on to the soul mans pulse light. Some of us need to come to terms with not wanting love, you can't love again. It's hurting you inside. Your heart is all broken up, and you can't give up because you don't have it in you from the beginning. Just like the song says, he's got the whole world in his hands. So let it go because he's got your whole heart in his hands and your problems as well. He buries them at the cross, so with a new song singing in his heart. Everything you own can be gone in a second, but your soul is still here standing in his glory. Let God paint you the big picture of the life he gave you. From the beginning, your future has been in his hands. Time is passing away, and this earth is not the end for you, only the beginning. Be a secret agent in the wide-open places of this world so that people can find the light. To give to the Lord one self I say, it has its moments for leading a person astray it has to be there choice to, maybe you had to bear your own cross to, so in detail you have to go throw life and survive from this world, you can be in it but not of this world.

You can't start a project and not finish. It is God's project. It is not for you to finish but for him to finish it in you, so keep going with the sword in hand. He's been working on it from the day you were born. Please do not get stone deaf here, people. Let the true self come out so God can use you. One can't rush things here. It takes time to get your game back in line. Find his voice once again. What must I do? There is nowhere to turn to. The one thing that comes up is my hiding place, which I know. No one knows where I am, that is when I take time to pray. Let him walk throughout the meadows, step-by-step. Keep yourself on that road. The more emptying the more it takes all of you, not part of you. To give up some things is the only part of what happens. If I can't see my way through, my dreams just fade away, why do I have to be responsible for my friends and family around me every single day? I try to take one day at a time. Who cares if it takes me a long time, are some years of my life to find that I am in the perfect will of God? Those things that you have a passion for, believe me, he knows them and he sees you in your desperate moments. People ask you what is your proof of purchase from God. You tell them that he lives inside of you and me, if he really dose, you can say that in your heart and in your soul. I tell you I can feel him all around me because I have been born again. What is born again it is when you ask the lord to forgive you of your sin's and ask him to save you and to come into your heart and the lord will do just that. Instantly you will be changed from the old you to a new born again you that you will feel different and you will think more clearly in a whole new way. I like to have a brand-new life. So try to live a sinless life. I try to be perfect, but only Jesus can make you perfect but this fleshly body can hold you back sometimes. When we get to heaven, there is no worrying about anything. Bear the image of Jesus Christ bleeding and dying for your sins. He purchased your soul for his keeping so that we all can walk and talk to him anytime anywhere we want. We build all our truths all around Jesus. Just remember what he said in the Holy Bible. He left a note for us to follow by in all his wisdom. He holds all the cards. He is putting living waters inside of us. And just remember the future is happening in front of your eyes. Sometimes, you will not notice it until some major event goes on at that moment. You cannot figure it out. This is only one way. It is not going to happen if you just sit and do nothing. Going on just being uneducated and poor that's call moving away from Gods plan for your life. And you know I am really sick and tired of the devil messing with me at night. He thinks we don't pray at night. Some do; some don't. So what are you complaining about? When trouble comes I really want to see that devil tremble when I throw out the holy scripture at him. He will say I can't mess with him he knows the Bible. The word of God, the devil can not stand it if you been born again and filled with the holy spirit, you can defect the devil the holy spirit is Gods power he give's us to live a sin free life yes indeed. As we get deeper in the Lord, in the right way, things that used to give us problems start to fade away, and at the same time God is teaching you his wisdom, not the wisdom you must figure out. It is very important to pray in your daily walk. In doing so, you will find yourself striving for the return to oneself by not giving up on your dreams. There is something to look forward to. You will have no more problems to deal with, but you will have to deal with problems but in a better way for some of us it maybe a trail that you must go though it may last a month, six months, or a year the lord always bring you out ok. It is up to you to strive, to seek his face more and more so that he will give you the desires of your heart. You feel that you have been labeled like a car sticker with an expiration date, things are going so fast that you don't know what hit you. You have not been taking time-out for yourself. Your spirit is crumbling like cookie crumbs, so who is going to pick up the pieces for you? Let the lord take care of your soul glow in your every step so that you can go through life meekly. Trust in him with that little bit of faith and strength that you have. Now you are running on Jesus power fuel now who is in charge of your day and week so get up and get you some cup of Jesus he will warm your soul up.

From any given moment, your soul can be taken over like a kidnapper taking you over with no feelings. Whatever you do, it is not working. So what's next, Mr. Big? You need to take it a day at a time. The one thing we all do not know is when Jesus Christ is coming. It can be at any moment, day or night, like a thief in the night.1 Thessalonians 4:13-18. 13. But I would not have you to be ignorant, brethren, concerning them which are asleep, that ye sorrow not, even as others which have no hope. 14. For it we believe that Jesus died and rose again, even so them also which sleep in Jesus will God bring with him. 15. For this we say unto you by the word of the Lord, that we which are alive and remain unto the coming of the Lord shall not prevent them which are asleep. 16. For the Lord himself shall descend from heaven with a shout, with the voice of the archangel, and with the trump of God: and the dead in Christ shall rise first:

17. Then we which are alive and remain shall be caught up together with them in the clouds, to meet the Lord in the air: and so shall we ever be with the Lord. 18. Wherefore comfort one another with these words. He will take you over with him for his purpose to heaven. We must do the things that Jesus asks us to do on this earth before we go on our trip to heaven. He just comes and goes with a purpose. He must reprogram our thinking to renew a right spirit in us, to clean up the temple our body's for the Holy Ghost, which is this fleshly body we are all living in. But the real person lives inside of us. We must take great care to bring out the fruits of the spirit by which are our praying lips. We make the choice to destroy ourselves. It is not God in the making. We are in the making, good or bad choices, and at the same time a lot of things are destroying the earth as we speak. When we lean to a different road in life at the same time, we are getting away from God's calling in our lives very quickly, without even noticing how bored we are feeling. We are not shaking up hell, not saying as much about our Lord and not affecting anybody in life. We need to keep walking away from the way we used to be. Feel kind of out of place not normal you are always in the midst of world affairs, which are not your own. So you shut down on your spirit life. Sometimes, you must give up something to lose another a little or a lot of yourself, and in the process, you gain peace of mind and hope and faith to go to the next level in God. It is in our nature not to give up on things that concern us. Our survival skills kick in, that extra strength within us, and that compels us to do our very best. Bad habits will stay with you for the rest of your natural life. You need to get those things out of your lives in the early stages, or they will become big problems later in life. The world has gone mad, and we are really living on the planet of the apes. It is in our nature to declare Marshal Law on ourselves. Some people use it for good; some use it for bad or in between for business, for learning, for shopping, or looking for the bad stuff, talking about, locking up your doors on this one. We do not know our limitations to hold. Our flesh, which is captive, and is crying out, "Feed me says your flesh, and you say, not today. Our flesh does not like the things of

God we all have a lot of work to do especially the Christians of today. There is a different kind out there, one crying out in the wilderness sold out for Jesus. While I lie awake in my bed, sometimes in the middle of the night, you can fall and really put the soul out of the box here. There is pain in the world. How many people are crying in the middle of the night like that? People are dying and going to hell out there somewhere, and the earth feels all this tension. A lot of stress and pressure is going on right now between the heavens and the earth. The only question is who is going, and who will be left behind a hard thing to say. But who is staying on this earth when Jesus come back to take us to heaven it will be those who have not except Jesus, the destruction of mankind, Such a desolate place it will be, a sad day, trouble on every hand, and great detachment to people it will be, you think we are all fighting for gas, water, food and finding shelter from the storm. And the one thing that is the most important your soul salvation, can you really make it though it all you really have a choice to make, take the mark of the beast, or beheaded for the cause of Christ, I'm saying it out loud and clear I do believe in Jesus. Have we forgotten the promises that Jesus said to his disciples? They believed when they saw him leave this earth and blessed the ones who had not seen him. But on some sweet day, to have all the hope of heaven in their souls, you feel the earth move in haste in that very moment.

You can feel that things are set in motion to set forth the saying that this nation is going and Jesus is coming soon. Some will repent; some will go a head fighting for what they believe in our self righteousness will not stand only what Jesus commands. It will all come to an end, to bring forth a new way of living, a new earth. To stand in his commandment to hear his voice though our heart and soul not with our mind that plays tricks on us sometimes we are always thinking on the things we don't have it is always a time and a place for all things it's ok. Psalm 37:4-5. 4. Delight thyself also in the lord; and he shall give thee the desires of thine heart. 5. Commit thy way unto the Lord; trust also in him; and he shall bring it to pass. To hold on to something we work hard for that feels good that nobody can not take it away from us. The world don't want you to have it and Jesus said it, he will give you the desires of your heart. Keep seeking his face everyday keeping the faith not giving up on yourself, the day, will come that a lot of people are going to see it the purest of hearts gives the most gifts out because to live a sinless life you have to give up your very own flesh that is the biggest enemy against us.

All the wants that your body curves, the world gives it to you before your eyes. You can't believe that all those things were in you, talking about a Christmas list. Your self-image ego is gone and replaced with Jesus Christ's image. People will see somebody else. Some people may stop you somewhere on the street or while you are shopping and may tell you that you are like there daddy back home, you are like his son, uncle, aunt, niece. The good in you shines on. It is not the boredom. It is the empty space between you and the real life. Give yourself a slap in the face. You are here, but you are not just going through the motions you know very well. You do not let yourself, go keep yourself organized as much as possible. You clean your car, house, bedroom, your outside lawn, and some people say you used up your gifts. Somehow, you are going crazy in your mind. You do not know what to do with yourself. You are running out of money, time, and you are all alone, all by yourself, and now what? You can take so much, asking yourself, "Does it matter or end?" But you know it is only the beginning. How do we determine what stays or what goes in our lives today? The good news is that we do have Jesus right now, and the world is getting crazier by the minute. The thing is that people just don't care about at all is your feelings. In their minds they say I am richer than you I'm smarter to. So bow down to me. I have a fancy car I have a great job, we are rising up a lot of takers in our time, and those smart people out there you do some pretty dumb stuff to, so with that said do we have the chance to reach this kind of people, "Yes" we do. If we, the last people standing let me rephrase that. The Christian people are all around and the things all around us are coming to an end you can feel it, time itself is speeding up. Very hard right now for me to deal with sin in my life I got to realize we need to wake up the sleepy giant in us.

Why do I have to be born in this kind of a world? We just can't live off our emotions. They will kill us from the inside out. The mind is playing tricks on you; you are starting to second guess yourself the things you are used to doing are going out on a date, and time is taken away. Throughout our lives, we always go mobile, with no direction at all. We work for longer hours in this lifetime. After a while, we become an item or a product of mass production. We cannot lose our minds. People today are losing time and are losing everything, including their jobs even after having worked twenty years or more. So that's the way it goes. In God's economy, like what the Bible says. Matthew 16:26-27. 26. For what is a man profited, if he shall gain the whole world, and lose his own soul? Or what shall a man give in exchange for his soul? 27. For the son of man shall come in the glory of his father with his angels; and then he shall reward every man according to his works. So take one day at a time with all this fast living it will break you down fast. I want to go to that quiet place with God, and I don't care what happens to me when I go there, with him. The burning love, which I have inside me for my Lord is the same thing I want for my future wife, and kids with a life long passion, a total surrender to God. And in that surrendering searching for that gift that is hiding inside of you the whole time do not hide your gift from yourself from the world that is not good so get back your worship switch same gears in your life get more time outs for yourself. And do some worshiping let God take you away, this is needed for discipline the gift that you have inside of you needs to be cultivated the things that we do in this world us the ones that make that choice for the good in God's way. It has to be a willing heart out there to hear the hurting calls of crying and suffering people a holy devoted individual, automatically the spiritual miracle spiral kicks in for that person. So who will answer to the call, Which is The Road Less Traveled.

He knows what to do when it is needed. In order for that to happen, he or she should be praying, watching, and reading their Bibles day and night. This is not a secret passion. It is open to the public freely to renew a right spirit within yourself. What is your secret which lies in every bedroom though out America your talents your gifts that are locked up dormant to the true self to unlocking that the light has come upon you a drop of knowledge from God an Ideal seems a crazy reaction to the body to act upon. It is a good thing to do this to benefit the sole purpose. You are that kind of a person who is always mad at the world that it keeps on throwing mud at you. You go through this for years, and finally something in life hits you like a ton of bricks, and now we have a soft spot to work with. Here my soul is crying out for more of you, to let it go. So that is your sole purpose: You keep on fighting the good fight. Can we celebrate life together in this book? Let him take control of the wheel to put you back on the right road, which is less traveled, to take you to that place with God and not the wrong place. For the ones in their bedrooms within that dark room, they have with them a lamp at their desk for spot light and to figure things out in their minds on a piece of paper. Just stop. Let God speak to your spirit. He will give it to you at the right time when you need him. Now come on now. How do you know who is waking you up at night? Is it an angel that wakes you up at night could it be the lord, waking you up in the still of the night to pray, sometimes he does that but he can't talk to you any other time because you are to busy all the time.

I say to you get on the right track with this, so go on with God and meet your future that only a few people have and are waiting upon. The lord will renew your strength you will mount up with wings as the eagles. Just the other night while getting ready to go to bed, I started thinking about the future if I had a family of my own a wife and kids. Can I really take on that responsibility, I will one of these days. "Could I really love someone?" Really, I am ready for this in life. Yes all the single people sometimes weary about this, and as for you I want to meet the right person for me, she has to love the lord as much as I do and love helping people. And if you are a Christian you would want this to, because a non believer would not understand why you love the things of God so much. I started thinking to myself that I am not alone the lord will guide you and strengthen you in your walk no matter what happens. Something in me stopped it from being a crying moment, time out. I put my mind on the things that the devil took out of my survival fight. You make the choice. You decide and what's not the real deal. I choose to hear the truth to move toward the right way of living. You got to remember the warning signs of life, and Jesus himself is shooting up blazes of flairs in to the sky. Looking up toward him, keeping eyes on him, you can see it. So wake up.

He is speaking to you throughout your daily living, through people, the radio, the Internet, the newspaper, and family members who are close to you. In that closeness with Jesus, sometimes the lord will wake me up at night I could be in a deep sleep and I hear a knocking at my door that's the lord waking me up to talk to him sometimes I feel my bed shake while still sleeping. In a deep sleep, in the middle of the night, I hear knocking at my bedroom door but I still hear it. Through my spirit, you are thinking to yourself, "Is this possible? Could this really happen to a person in this kind of state?" Yes, it can because it happened to me. Several different times in my life that I can remember, I wonder if this is one of the signs that Jesus is using, trying to tell us to not sleep and not slobber not playing with our soul like that and to disregard are denying self. Our number one enemy is this fleshly body. We are the temple of the Holy Ghost, but we will always have this fleshly body until we die. This is one of the main reasons that is plaguing us today. The first man who descended from Adam was created by God. You hear his calling in many different ways. God chose you to do a specific task in life. You are gifted to do that. So go on with God. Do it to find out the great mysteries that lie before you. That the love inside will carry you on to his perfect will that you are in right now, when I wake up in the morning for your guidance to your love a special kind of strength comes from God so I fix and put things in order for me to be blessed by him he washes away the tears from my eyes. Till this day you steel have the right recipe and the right ingredients for life, what to put in and what not to put in. The day that started is when the lord bought life to me from a praying mother who walked by faith, and I thank you lord for keeping my heart burning for you when I am all broken inside you come and fix me up my missing parts The real me was all over the place. I did not have a real father in the flesh at that time but you came to me and you loved on me and that made me feel good for me. I like the times we talk together lord in the mornings and in the afternoon and specially at night. Sometimes, it will be really late. You put my mind at peace. Lord you are teaching me to be a loving husband to my future wife, to be her all and all in my life. At this point, I have broken off so many things. Right now, the devil has been taking things from me for a very long time, and now the volcano has exploded. And it's squeezing me, stretching, and making me fall to the ground, and I am not getting up for a while. Where do I turn to, this is what I said back then in my life and it seems to be out of desperation. And God, I know that you are taking care of the lonely people of the world, especially with the earthquakes of the world. I am praying for them as well as my own people. Our core convictions are so many that they develop with us. We reject the more a different side of beliefs, which were handed out to us early in life. Some people find out too late on the basics of life that we model after we plan and make decisions, interrupting people's lives and their actions toward God. We try making meaning out of our life's experiences, solving problems, patterning ourselves to relationships with others, working hard to stay straight, developing our careers, making a plan of action to establish priorities that are right for you and your family. By making all these decisions for your faith in Jesus, did you forget about the fact that when a person do hears the words of Jesus it speaks in his or her heart, they need to believe and the treasure the real truth inside will stay with them for the rest of their lives. Usually, a person will need to hear the word of God minster to them regularly from church or from a bible study group to develop a new worldview, a new, clear sharp view for which we usually have to be much thankful for. At this point, this usually takes the form of both praying and seeking God for yourself. Even singing a new song to God. So the more you see or go through your life, the more thankful you will be about your past experience. You are learning something before your time, so what do we do about that? You cannot throw it away, are it stays with you for the rest of your life. That is the gift that God put in you, so go on. You made it this far. This is only the beginning of things to come, so do the things that you love to do. The automatic love that lives in all kinds of weather, even in your darkest hour to see it in your hands, it speaks for itself. Just see the many wrinkles, cracks, sores, blisters, cuts, bloodshots, the mud in between your fingernails in your hands. You try fixing on stuff, trying to survive one more day gracefully. And all the problems of the world seem to go away when you go to bed at night. The relief that you feel in your mind, picking out the moments of the day, when you lay this old sinful body down is good for you. So you run with that in your mind. Now you tell me who is running the remote control and who is handling the joystick of air traffic control? Do we have a problem with this part of the scene in life? Do you want to be loved? Do you want the pathway that belongs to you its closer than you think? To explain this, just say a prayer to your self, say my God can do those things and he does not forget them. And stop saying to yourself that God forgot about you. The language you use to cry out to God, were in complaints, of unbelief in the midst of our suffering, we won't out of it quick in the event that it always, leads us up to a conversation with God. He is the only first resort not your last in all of this. When the hard times come, I know that God really loves me, even in the bad times. Try to be sensitive to God's sole best interest, you are not ready for him to change you and your whole family.

It is a cool cloudy day hear at the park I hear birds singing, the squirrels playing in the trees, the wind blowing. It is really peaceful. It is a very woody forest like place. Anybody can run here just to get away from all the noisy stuff of life. This is one of the places from where I start writing. I thank Jesus Christ for all of this nature it is beautiful. Right now, I never go far from home because home is where the heart is. Just take off your shoes and give them to me. I will walk a mile for you. Why do we say that because of love in the heart and for some no love, peace, happiness, and unity, and that you couldn't come on time for dinner? Will somebody lift a plate for you? Can you really give thanks to the wives, husbands, the moms and dads, the sons and daughters, the grandmas, the grandpas, the single moms, the single dads? Just a little something goes a long way. To underline the stress factory, not getting in with the devil that is a question for any Christian who wants to practice being the church instead of just attending, one should pay attention to the signs of the time to pay attention to your surroundings for once. For some, the typical story of life might be a bit too hard to follow. Take those chances along, which I have missed, for people of all walks of life. Most of them can find their answer in other things the creative people to find out is God out there for some to find the road less travel with the bible. And you are thirsty for your choices. Find the answer to your problems that is the question at your soul finger tips.

If we don't pursue our passion, the things that you love to do, that big something important won't happen, and God wants you to be happy. I call the snapshots of life that were lost "your soul brain." This is just an example for that note from all the information stored in your brain can not compare to what's in your soul, it has two different kinds of scenarios here the mind can only remember people, places and things. But the soul feels the moment which can take you there for that time, making you feel good to and all over in that is a close in counter with your god in worshiping in singing and dancing in the spirit in that full contact in your praying, and kneeling on the side of your bed all real no magic tricks here. We all need to take time for ourselves, to let our soul be free and not stuffed in a pillowcase. This will put the body at rest. Don't think about anything but the Lord. You may be really mad at the world. But in all, it's trickery, evil stuff. When is enough is enough all ways picking up people's dog pup and really feeling mad sick inside this uncomfortable anger inside of you believe me it will try to control you like going insane. I just got to be real here a grown man that works hard every day and broke as hell the bank charging overdraft fees on your checking account your car payment is due for two or three months and missing up your body with these quickies at these fast food places do you really know what you want in life.

Is it worth killing yourself for low wage jobs, working fourteen to sixteen hours a day? If you are really still reading this book, you are doing good so far. You are the kind of person who wants to be blessed in your soul, also in life. It is not wrong to have something that you worked long and hard for and wanting and waiting for your heart's desirers. This is one of the reasons why I am writing this kind of book for those kind of people who have been pushed in a corner in that wall of shame. Now tell me, is it worth it to wake up in the morning, saying thank you, Jesus for one more day of air to breathe, to see the sun rise in the morning, to hear the birds sing, to hear the wind blow from the top of the swinging trees? You got to get caught up in this, people. Believe it, to help your soul benefit in the long run, we must fall in love with Jesus with all our heart and let him sanctify you in a renewed spirit. A sweet smelling, sacrifice acceptable, well pleasing to God the worship out from your mouth from your soul. You did all you could. So it just feels like someone tied your hands behind you, made you stand up, turned you around, and took you to the corner of the room with your face turned to the white pale wall, and there you are just staring at that for the rest of your life. Time is just passing you by. And I can't keep up. I am too slow at times, too weak some times, and because of my sin, I keep on doing it every day. I can't stop this; it is eating me up inside. Let me out of here, Jesus. Help me not to go through the same routine every day.

Even on my off days of work, I am off-balance and not in touch with family events or issues. All I am thinking about is the next day. There is no peace in my mind, body, and soul. If I wanted to go somewhere it would be really good for me, I don't have the money right now to go to release my stress. When I had the money, I was too tired to go, or something comes up to destroy my downtime with myself and the Lord. Just do it without thinking, and let him talk to you about where to go from here. It feels like you have been doing a lot of sinning these days. Well, the sin that you are doing maybe a small or a big sin. Well, I have to tell you, sin is sin big or small. It doesn't matter. Whatever it is, it will send you to hell. On the questions to be asked it is your choice to repeat of your sins now or later it goes for the Christians who back slide, and the non-believers to repeat now you cannot play games with your soul. All should come with a willing heart to come subjection he is calling you, do you hear his voice in the middle of the night, is it going straight to your very soul so get up out of your set and lift up your hands to the sky, if you can it doesn't matter where you are, and say. Dear Jesus Christ come in to my heart right now lord.

Just remember that you were trained for this. In your whole life, you were taught to fight, taught to talk to the masses of people, taught to sing to them not at them, with a new song, taught to walk this life without falling down on yourself. You did not even know that you were going backward this whole time. It's OK not remembering that you have a family that loves you a lot. So please do not put your back to a corner. If you must do it were to focus all your momentum that has been building up in you all in these times of training trust in him not your feelings what does your heart and soul tell you in case of emergency bailout. The other day Jesus told me leading up till today, then it starts to kick in your time with the lord in that closet now pick up your sword and start killing some devils. Now if you want to know yourself better, get to know your Creator, the Molder, the Shaper. When Jesus speaks to you, listen to him. He will give you the answer to your troubles; maybe you are not at a place were you wont to be, so keep moving on toward your future. When the fiery darts of life come at you like a flood, be unmovable like a tree planted by the living waters of life as mentioned in Psalm 23:2, "He maketh me to lie down in green pastures: he leadeth me beside the still waters." You've got to trust in him. I have to say it. When you are in the deepest trouble, you get the best revelations. It speaks out louder than words. We are deceiving our own self it is so exhausting like baring waste land I keep saying to myself I can't believe this is happening to me today sometimes you do not want to see the sun shining that day you would like to see a cloudy window instead of a sunny window.

Oh, please give me a cloud. I am telling you. Do not give the devil the real original recipe of the real you. It is your choice to make it. There is no place or any room for the devil to get in my life. All the rooms go to Jesus Christ. Never say when you are praying that you have nothing else to say and that you feel you have run out of words to say. This is one of the real things. What does your soul say? It says, "I want Jesus now in my life if you have nothing to say then give him thanks. Do no more empty praying, we need to take care of our spiritual life. Keep that balance on, not off. It is like splashing my life's work on my bedroom walls with all the colors of the rainbow. I have been doing so for a number of years and now finally completed. A firm action came over me, and then I stopped everything that I was doing. Then I grabbed a bucket of white paint that was left over from last year's little projects and started to paint over the really colorful wall with this white paint without thinking of it. It took me a very long time to do. And I felt no pain inside me, so I continued on painting the walls and almost finished. I got to think. I cannot go back because it won't be the same again because something in me has changed for the better. Those colors that I had in the past on the walls have changed. God was telling me to clean my life up and to make it whiter than snow. Now those colors are purified with my forgiveness, with joy, and peace of mind, and everything is going to be fine.

Let me drop some word of knowledge in this day, in the age were the computer is trying to beat the human brain. With the iPod and now the iPad, and with a light touch of your finger on the screen, you can flap a page without physically touching the book itself. And now going with the mind of remembering stuff that happen twenty even forty years ago back logging like files stored in the back of the mind just like that it can break the computer in half just remembering the days back then and time and the year that you got saved the mind itself is a time traveling machine if it was just yesterday. People think that you are strange sometimes, or you have been misunderstood, but somehow you are gifted. You are stuck in a bad life you are living in. The good stuff in your life is the blessing. You went to the next guy who passed you by, thought to yourself, "This could not be for me, man." It sure feels like I'm going though the meat grounder of life hear, oh God you got to get me out of here. I can't live without you, Lord. I do not know how I landed on the ground, and I am still on the ground for a very long time. Help me, up Lord. I don't want to block this road of separation. I just can't keep it to myself. I have to tell somebody my soul is talking to you like the way I keep taking to God in my prayer time. I can express myself more on paper. I am not a songwriter or a screenwriter for movies. This is straight from god are you still trying to figure God out, and your own life out? Are you trying to figure out the meaning of all this? Sometimes, it feels like I was supposed to be in someplace in my life. My choice and my timing is off here the thing I did not do like hitting the knees. What I mean is I got on my knees at times to pray.

I am not finding out what God has for me, he has plans for me, so I sit back and wait until he shows me and at the some time trying to solve the puzzle. No matter what level you are in your spiritual walk, life has to keep going. Your age or your high position in the business world does not matter. The standpoint of the government is, if you are rich or poor does not matter. Neither your race or where you are living at or what kind of bed you are sleeping in it doesn't matter. The Lord Jesus is always going to bring you to him no matter what. And you think he forgot. He keeps on bringing you back to school with the Bible. You cannot run away from him, and God knows the second you make that decision. For those who have made the choice to live for Jesus forever, your word is your bond from your soul. Heaven is your home. This world will fail you but not God. He will never leave you or forsake you. His voice is right by your side closer than your own brother so that your soul lives longer and prospers. As you are walking through your life in this book, there will be changes. Changes will come about. You will know it by now when my words start to change as weeks and months and even years go by. I will grow older with time, and this book will be my living legacy to my generation. To have come to this point, I did not have a background to have written a book like this. With such motivation in me, I am growing stronger every day in my life. Please do not stop reading this book. This is only the beginning, and now let me go through my life and see what level God is going to take me through. I think that some of you, still need this to day, and you are scared of the dark. You leave on a night-light or a small lamp in your bedroom, or it could be some unfinished unique business of your childhood leading up to your adulthood. So what's the problem here? I hear that the devil stole your childhood from you. And you are still carrying about that thing today in you for the rest of your life and putting that incident in the back of your mind like shopping online. You are not buying the product or item now, but you are saving it. When you have more money, you saved up. And say to your self, "This is who I am. So they call me a loser. God made me and put me on this earth for a reason. It is for me to figure it out for myself." So keep on living. He knows that you are trying your best, so give him a try. Jesus is the answer to all your problems; it is his way, not your way.

You got to keep the rhythm of balance on your own. It is your choice to make it like a professional boxer when he jumps rope. It keeps him on his toes; along with that goes his rhythm, his balance to move with grace. The ring helps him to focus his eyes on his opponent and organize anger within his self. It is like that with the devil trying to get you, keep on watching and praying. And at the same time, he is watching from a far off place, preying on you for your weak spots. But you are strong in battle, and you have the purest of heart. To give up one's need is to wait on God on some things, to hope on some things greater than your self just like a man. Desiring a woman so it is like desiring God's love for me. Because he changed me from all those desires but I keep them down under the blood of Jesus. You know we single guys have a desire for a woman but God helps us though his power to overcome those feelings until its time for your future wife. I wonder what I will learn from the look in her eyes. I wonder what I will see in the color of her eyes. I see the wonderful design that God had made, speaking loving words to her to my future wife. I see a tear roll down her cheek. Lord Jesus, I see her tears coming down I will say to my self I have touched her heart. So I have the freedom to speak to the lord whatever is on my mind and spirit, and if I have a questions to ask of him. That will help me to find the way. I know right now that I have a burning passion for love. I know it is good to cry, but sometimes I just hate myself for not making my move on a dream. Yes, I do regret it. That's my human emotion to have the mind-set to reset button of my soul. Now is not the time to quit right now I am in a holding tank a prisoner over my soul? I am in my own, in a world all by myself. I don't see you, but I feel you in the middle of my stomach. That tells me it is not me; it is he leading me onto those open doors of my soul. I reach out my hands toward you, Lord, and I am calling out your name. Jesus, help me. I don't know if I am the only one who does this. But I try to create something for myself. I am dwelling in a secret place, in the highest place. I have no more tears on my face. I am hungry for your love. Lord you are the only one who can take this pain away from my heart. Speak to me again, Jesus. I need your voice to guide me through my cloudy eyes. I am feeling so much better talking to you. Face-to-face with you in this book, you are helping me onto my victory and to help people. We cannot afford to stop talking to Jesus. We can't live day after day with out praying. You are killing your soul man, the Bible is our food and water of life. You need to grow in his image. If things in your life are going wrong, there is always an end to the problem that you are facing, and quit saying to yourself, "Who am I?" Until you knew you took a chance on it, in front of your face, a second chance to wake up in the morning to breathe again to see the sun on my face Jesus you have turn me inside out a change that will bring a change on the out warded apparents. That's why people say there is a glow about you a shine and there it comes a beckon in the darkness to find your way back home to Jesus.

You may find yourself crying inside. Yes, your soul seems to have no love, peace, or a voice to hear. Jesus's voice is there. Yes, you can talk to your soul like no other person can. Think how it is going to be in heaven itself. Go beyond yourself in worship. It is fresh on your soul to remember the first time you met Jesus, feeling his sweet precious glory. He set your heart on fire, and your face was filled with joy, peace, and with tears of happiness. Yes, I think that I am taking you there. It is a place worth fighting for that kind of level can really take you to places you have never been before. I tell you, I choose to listen to him. The actions I do are guided and ordered by him only. Wow! Man, I am telling you right now. Sure, it is hard right now at my standpoint. Lord, what's the point of all this? My body is tired, and my mind is somewhere else. I am not focused now. Days come and go like a fast-forward time machine. I am telling you, a lot of God's grace is still here that is living, walking, standing, working, playing with your children and even with those who rejected him for their past sins. So you hide yourself, but he sees everything. He is a very big God. And with that mind-set, I dare you to believe in God who takes captive of this house. To know god and how he do things in the spirit rime. In real wisdom, he knows how to keep his house in order and to build. Seek him in that passion and try not to fear. Things can change in your life. Believe in him to strip you from everything. Just lift your head up to him to see the big picture, and that's what he is doing with me right now to teach me to breathe in his presence. Strive to change. I know it seems foreign to you. It makes you feel like you don't know how to read. Only when you push yourself, the revolution comes. And when the light comes on it is as if you were in a state of sleep, when was the last time you just really lose you, oh man Jesus this is talking to me right now like a big prize at Christmas can't hardly wait.

There are still people waiting on Jesus, which is a good thing to do, but the truth it is, the other way around. Jesus is waiting on them and the ones who think Jesus really left them high and dry, are saying to themselves, "I am losing hope here. I feel like I slipped off the edge, of the cliff, and. I am falling in to a bottomless of nothing." I do not have anything to show for it. I have no backups, no plan A or plan B. It is just me feeling so sorry for myself. I need a Jesus plan of action. Right now, I am tired of making sequels. I want to move in God's direction in my life why 40 has to be a near death experience with yourself just to find yourself to come back again stop keeping your sins for a rainy day and know it don't feel good right now back to your own dodo. Isaiah 40: 30-31 says. 30. Even the youths shall faint and be weary, and the young men shall utterly fall: 31. But they that wait upon the Lord shall renew their strength; they shall mount up with wings as eagles; they shall run, and not be weary; and they shall walk, and not faint. Psalm 37: 5-8 says this. 5. Commit thy way unto the Lord; trust also in him; and he shall bring it to pass. 6. And he shall bring forth thy righteousness as the light, and thy judgment as the noonday. 7. Rest in the Lord, and wait patiently for him: fret not thyself because of him who prospereth in his way, because of the man who bringeth wicked devices to pass. 8. Cease from anger, and forsake wrath: fret not thyself in any wise to do evil. I want to seek out after that peace that passes all understanding. Dare to move dare to learn from God act on your soul we need to take care that which is near dear to our hearts oh please don't give up now for I am scared to try something new do it for a change. Did I plan this to happen to me at this time? It is really a bad timing, a big fat slap in the face. Folks, in a matter of two months and half, you may go without a job or money. All your backups are gone, and now your health and life is on the same line as a single man who is almost reaching his late thirties. And I suppose he is in the prime of his life. I am trying to get up right now. I really feel dazed and confused, and for the last five years I had been on the top of my game, with a really good job for the first time of my life. I got it down packed, and it seems so well now. God says it is time to wake up, boy. I made many bad choices. I can't really blame God for this. I feel like I am all alone. It is very easy to get to my soul; it has been cut open to let everybody know that I can bleed too, like a museum on display. I can lose my mind, but I don't have it in me to go that way, for some people choose that route, not me. So how much stress can you handle by saying to yourself that if anything happens to you, you will go crazy? This is uncommon to me like a freak accident on the freeway. So many things in life are coming at you, all at once. Right now, I feel that I am in a real dry place with myself. I feel like giving up, but that still small voice inside of me is saying like we sing, we fall down, we get up. We all need some kind of motivation from somewhere. It is a long road to pull back the curtains to my victory and hope in Jesus style. If you really want to know how sick this world is, just sit in the waiting room of a hospital all day. You will see people from all walks of life, from all races, from the babes to the old folks. There are tall people and short people; there are skinny people, heavyset people. Everybody is talking differently, and you think you are the only clean Christian person who just came out of nowhere. So you come back to yourself, saying, "I think God is trying to talk to me in a different kind of way." We don't get it until everything we own is all gone in the blink of an eye, trying to figure it out in our own mind. It keeps on giving me a clean slate. Oops! Did I just break out of my shell to reveal my own very soul that had been "Wi-Fi," hooked up with my God who keeps on bringing heaven to my life? Now it is time to seek God with all my heart and with all my soul. It is not for me to go the wrong way with myself, to put all my skills, all my knowledge, all my wisdom that God gave throughout the years in one basket. I know that I can do this because I wasn't by myself when I was preaching in the schoolyard when I was a kid. I just remember that my voice bounced off those brick walls, and I did not have a Mick phone then, just me and my God. Yes" when I was in the third grade I knew the things of God my father is Evangelist I learn about God from him and my mother and I got the fire he had back when I was a little boy I saw him preach the love of God to many people his compassion and love for the people, and now he work's with Christian Radio Programs. And my mother told me to sure Jesus with the kids if they picked on me and when I did that one kid ask me are you a preacher and that's how I got the name preacher boy. And now writing this book is wonderful. I do not know what the future may bring, so live day by day. I had to let a lot of things go so that God can use me better. There are too many things rolling in my mind, but my soul is not at rest at this point. There is something in me telling me that I have something to do in this life.

I have not been able to figure it all out. I have no more questions to ask the lord at this time. Jesus is still to this day teaching people to live the winning walk. Some people stumble off their road. Some fall, walk off their way, thinking that something got in their way, and that is slowing them down. There are so many devils, and so many levels to kill a devil. It all depends on you and on what chapter or what stage of life you are in. You could have experienced so many sleepless nights, gasping for the last fresh air, drowning in your own bed of self-pity, fearing that somebody is out to get you or trying to eat away at your sleep. Stay away from your problems. As soon as God starts to bless you, the devil wants to stick his big head in the middle, saying, "Give me the piece of the pie, yeh!" Then be in debt for the rest of your life, along with your credit cards too. So I am trying to say the truth on paper here that we always avoid the bullets of confrontation by just saying to ourselves, "Am I still myself who always put myself in front just to stay afloat by not saying anything, with no expression but with a stone cold face, with no feelings and with both hands in my pockets, always standing close by?" But you disappear somewhere. They call it a "stand-alone." But I try getting back my game face that I had once for five years, but now it feels like a meteor that has fallen from outer space and landed on me. It is a direct hit to my mind and body. I am still there, but I am weakening. I would like to be strong for my Jesus, but we are living in this fleshly body. You really have to fast and pray to stay full of the power of God. I tell you that Jesus is one tough act to follow. It makes me want to be more like him, so that keeps me going on with the plan to follow. So let's follow you on that hard road of life. We all will have bumps, cuts, and bruises. We should not put our gifts on the shelves. By doing that, it starts to collect dust from not using them for a very long time. You see, I cannot travel on your road. Everybody has to travel on their own road. Some people like to have shortcuts in life. It does not work like that. There is a saying that you carry your own cross, and there is only one way to heaven. I am tired of being burned out of time. I am not afraid. I just want to get stronger in the Lord's army. There is a time and place for everything. You must get your peace of mind. Try to do something different every day. It is your God-given to pursue a happier soul. While pursuing a happier soul, we keep on jumping over that fence, always running out of control, not stopping and taking a good look around. You see the warning signs of life closing in on you like the air pressure, sucking all the air out of you, trying to hold you. So, tighten up your belt. Please keep your mind clear and your soul grounded. I tell you one thing. You cannot be worried about stuff, and your problems. It starts to become a cancer, sucking all the energy from your body, and you can't think straight. You try to sleep it off but that don't work. You try to flush it out and It works for a bit, but it starts right back up. Life is a roller coaster. One minute, you have money, and a couple of hours later, you are broke, always paying on something. It is like a crime scene inside your mind. It seems like you are always falling into a police report with your sin and your soul always repeating why do I keep falling for the same trick.

I think feeling better consciously is more on the mind and the body. Than anything we like freedom, a state of mind. If I try to do just that, maybe I will lose weight faster. You must find your body the right combination to get back in shape. So it is with our finances that the lord will show us the right combination. It is your lifeline between you and your God. You must get out and do something you have never done before get out of your element. Make a difference in somebody's life. You will feel a whole lot better. Going out of town is the cheap way. Keep those roads going for yourself, if you could let yourself go like that. Keep on saying that time will make a comeback. I do not want to feel sorry for myself. Someone has to keep looking for a way out. Where is the exit? I am telling the truth here. I am not quitting on myself these days. I know things around are changing for the better in my life and in my family. Only God knows what's next for me. I am just here for the ride. Keeping your mouth shut is not the right way. Your gifts inside will make room for you to spread your wings like eagles flying in those clear blue skys. It seems they are trying to tell the truth, but they don't believe you. They are not a freak of nature but a Jesus freak for life. But what they say to you is to keep on the good fight. Just tell me lord if they don't believe in you, I'm more and more becoming like Jesus letting him mold me.

Walk in the light as he is the light. When you are walking on your road, keep a word. Memorize some scripture verses from the Bible, say them out of your mouth and in your very heart and soul. It has to be retained in your heart and in your mind within your gut you know this is right. Lord, guide me as a light unto thy path, guiding me through this dark world. Then I will fear no evil. Your fleshly body may die but your soul lives on it goes back to heaven. You may be crying on your road. You may feel lonely right now. He is giving you a second chance. Take it when you are all messed up inside, and all cut up inside and left for dead, but somehow you manage to put both hands on the ground. Both arms are bending to lift yourself up. Like a boxer in the ring, you still have got more fights. There is one more round to go. Commit an act of sacrifice and praise the Lord. You are in the perfect will of God. Do not worry about your future because you are stepping in it every day. Whenever a day passes, find yourself on top of the mountain and feel free to dream of your passions. I am not afraid that I have been through this path once before. You feel worried inside off your game and the red lights blinking really fast. You always find yourself worrying over losing a job and starting a new one in the same year or losing friends and not finding friends are a husband in a years span. You have a clean car inside, but your closet is still dirty, or you have a cloudy dark rainy day and a cold grumpy altitude. You are in a kind of world where there is a hot or a cool breeze or a sunny day with blue skies. I tell you one thing. God is the best weatherman in the galaxy. In saying that, we cannot separate ourselves from his love for us by keeping our mouth shut and not speaking to him. It is like not speaking to a wife when she keeps on telling her husband or boyfriend to please talk to me. When times get tough, he is the first and last person you should talk to when everything is gone from your life. I mean everything down to the clothes on your back. Yes, I said it, and that thing you are feeling right now I know is like there is nothing in the air. Colossians 1:9-11. says this. 9. For this cause we also, since the day we heard it, do not cease to pray for you, and to desire that ye might be filled with the knowledge of his will in all wisdom and spiritual understanding. 10. That ye might walk worthy of the Lord unto all pleasing, being fruitful in every good work, and increasing in the knowledge of God; 11. Strengthened with all might, according to his glorious power, unto all patience and longsuffering with joyfulness. Go ahead and reach out your hand to that in which you are feeling nothing. You may feel like an outcast who is out of place or out of control. On some days, you just don't feel like praying or speaking to anyone. He is taking you to that dry place with your fleshly body that is hurting you inside and out, purifying you, making you a different person when everything is gone from your life. You don't feel like washing your face or combing your hair. You may be wearing the same clothes for days at a time. You may have a lot of sleepless nights with no energy to do anything. Time is passing you by. You see day and night like a time machine going fast forward and can't do anything about it, feeling worried inside, and off and the only time you get is to go to the bathroom.

Do you want to know, why people like pain and suffering so much because it gets anxious for not changing. So they swim in it for months and years or even for the rest of their lives? They want someone to feel sorry for them and they are in sorry surroundings, and you, mite as well hide behind those brick walls of solitude, always saying to yourself, "Forgive me of my sins, "Stop that" because you do not want to change which I have done in the past and will not do in the future." I know that God has the book of life. He knows which of you are going to heaven and who's keeping up tabs on the devil's inventory of souls who are in hell with him? We hate this part of the story. We must win this war against sin and wrong doing, and not at the people's expense. We have to be spiritual connected with Jesus. Let him put his hands into your soul, and he will guide your soul on the right track. One of the things that gets me the most is when Christian people do not use what God gave them: their gifts and their talents. Watching them year after year, never changing for the better sounds very tempting to join in, but it is not my taste. It is like letting the water holes go on running out in the grass all day. That water is going to be wasted. Who cares? We have only one life to live. Can I be really delivered from my pet sin that I keep on doing three or four times a week? Yes so who's keeping up on your sin scoreboard? Let me tell you something. God knows everything we do on a daily basis. No one need to know that the "devil" did it to me I suppose to kill that sucker once and for all, with the word of God.

I do not accept whatever he tells me to do. I welcome the Lord in my life. For the choices that I make, we will pay for it sooner are later. We let him in to do our jobs. Family is in our minds. We carry our money over to our bedrooms. Believe it or not, God can take you to a dry place in your life from where everything would have been taken from you. So what was it your childhood are your teen age years are even to your 20's that something damaging can carry over to your 30's and 40's like that car crash commercials dummies you can learn a lot from a dummy just like, you can really lose control for the first time in your life, being afraid of yourself. I don't care about this world. It has too many problems in it. But one thing we must not do is pick up pieces from behind us from the past. It maybe sometimes you may have to go back and pick up in order to go on, that's find, but move on. Every time a problem comes up in the present, wow, I can be my own Christian team. We cannot con our way to heaven like a rich person would say, "I am going to buy heaven when I die." Getting some real estate and lots of money in saying that, there is a v.i.p seating in the hot seat waiting for him in hell, in the owner's box down in the lake of fire, if it was up to us we can lose our minds in the process fighting to survive we put everything else in but not putting Jesus in your everyday life or business we cannot push out God we all need is some vitamin protein for the soul. There are no vacations or rain checks to put your soul on hold. I will do it tomorrow. So you're telling me this is why people like to see fighting and violence in movies and music videos and making it look very good like lobster dinner switching up things in our minds the evil for good and good for evil is that the real culture of today.

Well I'm afraid that some parents today are letting their kids go and see very violent movies, which show sex acts. Kids are learning from this at a very young age. It is feeding the flesh in all kinds of ways. We need to let our kids see adventure movies family friendly movies, this is needed for the growing youth of today. This is causing self-destruction to private property. We lock away ourselves in our bedrooms from the kids we don't pay close attention to our kids like we should for days at a time. We are sick and tired of people, and there are ways of doing things putting there kids in harms way. Taking them to the liquor store with them and actual going in together that's really putting your souls on the back burner, you young teens of today does not talk to your parents on a regular basis who live with you under the same roof and you say to them, "I do not want to talk to you today." Days after that, you feel all kinds of pain inside, and you try to sleep it off by popping pain pills. You have an excuse of not talking to Jesus so only some of you call on him only when trouble come knocking at your door. So what's holding you back? Throw in your life jacket because you are drowning in your self-pity. You are in bad shape right now. You put yourself in prison, locking yourself away from your family, your best friend, your wife, your husband. Can I be a part of the crowd? I don't finish some things that I have started. You can't half finish a roof of a house. Eventually, that roof is going to start leaking when the rain starts to come. So are you a rainy kind of person, always letting bad stuff in and not sealing up or protecting your soul from the air pressure of life, and what I mean by air pressure of life while life is hard you can feel it in the air that's what I mean. Your choices will catch up with you. You tell yourself, "I need love right now." I feel so lonely right now for the single people out there, and for the shy ones I have a word of advice, "Be yourself. And the shy single people stop selling yourself short go pass the shyness, you're ok. You have something to say you say it, and open "Up" go for it this is your last chance. Quit letting it run through your mind." Love will find you, keep doing the right thing stay prayerful tell the Lord your feelings of loneliness some how some way before you know it. The Lord steps into the spool of those feelings and takes them away he is your friend. It has to come from your heart and soul to achieve greatness in your life. If you slip up in some sin, repent of it and move on. I know it feels like going to hell. That is the devil talking to you, exposing yourself like a car without a hood where all the elements of the world, the hot sun, the cold of winter, snow, and heavy rain pour down. Please make that choice of being on Jesus side. If you did move on that act by all means, come quickly and jump the fence if you have to. We all will find our way back home even if you move out of your mom and dad's house so how long has it been 10, 20 years sense you moved out. If your parents are still living, go to them. Let them know you love them, and say to them that they did a great Job of raising you. Life makes us teachers. It is in all of us. It comes now or later in life in many different ways. You say to yourself, "I can take it." Throw away those kid toys. This is the real ideal time to grow up to manhood and womanhood. But we still have to leave a light on in our bedrooms. Why is that a small night-light is plugged in to our wall? Are we still holding on to something that happened in our childhood stage? Boy, that past really kicks in when you are trying to go to bed, pulling that thick blanket over your head, thinking that it is going to protect you all night. You think that a big huge blanket can protect you from that. Something is going to grab you out of your bed or when you are in a deep sleep, tossing and turning and having a very bad nightmare. In the middle of the night, you wake up in a cold sweat or you wet the bed, saying, "What do I have to say?" There are a large number of adults who still do this to day wet the bed. It seems that anybody don't want to talk about it like saying we have flu problem don't worry we have it in containment we are fear filled people like I said this is a really big problem for some adults living in silence going the extra mile every morning this is not normal. It says 2 Timothy 1:7, For god hath not given us the spirit of fear but of power, and of love, and of a sound mind. The moment you feel that your health is coming back to you, save it for a rainy day. You are going to need it till the last drop of your spirit. All of you have a sword at hand at all times, watching and praying. Never let your guard down. Always staying up; sometimes, eye vision alone is not enough.

Your spirit is the one that feels and senses things around you. If you are ever going to use that sword, I'm talking about the Bible, Hebrews 4:12 says this. 12. For the word of God is quick, and powerful, and sharper than any twoedged sword, piercing even to the dividing asunder of soul and spirit, and of the joints and marrow, and is a discerner of the thoughts and intents of the heart. It is for those who have a willing heart. The characteristic of the real you come out. The only thing that is helping you out is that still calm voice in the middle of the night when Jesus says to you something by calling out your name. I am here to tell you when to grab the window of opportunity, which is knocking at your soul's door. I say that your soul moves faster than your flesh. It can't keep up with time or react. I am so sick and tired of crying for people who have no common sense, no sense of what is going on around them even though they are Christians but rookies in the faith. But they won't give up. We do make the choice of chapters in our life, which come to us automatically. But sometimes, we get to hide ourselves. The sense of urgency of skipping chapters of servile mode has been turned on, and you are left alone in a desert land in your mind. Who is writing the screenplay for our lives today? Stop and listen to the battle cry of the saints of God that their hearts are ready for his voice commanding that there hearts be filled with no fear of tomorrow and that your ears may hear the words of Jesus voice speaking to you every moment of the day. When you are eating, sleeping, using the computer, your laptops, your iPhones, iPads, or when you are playing with your kids, you will know that the time has come. Spend time with Jesus alone to do his work in you while we are waiting for God to call us home. The time and season to exchange hands and the time to reap the benefits is about to come. A spiritual spring-cleaning is here in your face. Yes, the devil knows how to kick and throw dust and dirt in your eyes. He sees that you do not see your way through your problem. Just take the next small step. Everything can change in a blink of an eye, but don't worry. God never blinks. He can do anything he wants. Let him help you. I maybe weak, but he is strong. So go on after what you love to do in life. Don't take no for an answer. It would be better to try and fail than just stay at home and never try, you need to pursue your dreams and visions and goals whatever God has in place in your heart. Maybe some of your best friends said that your mind won't be able to handle it, that you are slow in the mind, you have not gone to school, or that you will not make the grade in life. So I say, make peace with your past so that it won't screw up the present. I am so sick and tired of relatives trying to change you, are convert you. You must shave your hair, put this ring on your finger. What is the next fad for today's menu crowd out there.

In this case, life is too short to waste time hating anyone. It maybe ten or twenty years when you see that person again. By then, you will be too old to remember. No one else is in charge of your happiness but you. There are no sad songs, no sad movies, no sad news from the TV or from some of your friends. Believe in yourself. Believe in miracles. Step out in faith. He will do the rest. The best is yet to come. Life isn't tied with a bow, but it's still a gift in many different ways. The sun is shining today. I woke up this morning with air in my lungs. I have all five senses with me. I have faith in God that he will make away for my bills to be paid. My car is working fine for now. I know that the fact still remains. I have to make it to heaven. You are born here. You die here, but when God comes, you do not have to fall. Death is coming to you, trying to make a stand with yourself. It is a good thing. Just show up and be ready. Don't quit. You can succeed through pain and suffering. It is not you shaping yourself. God is shaping you. You have to get to that Promised Land. This is spiritual justice at hand here. You maybe feeling sick in your body, your arms, hands, fingers, legs, feet, upper, middle, and lower back or in your mouth, eyes, nose, ears, skull, brain, heart, lungs, ribs, stomach, kidneys, the large and small intestines, bladder, pancreas, the sexual organs, and so forth.

Everything comes to a balance sooner or later. Show forth your sword, and Jesus for all to see for that person, in him or her life lord Jesus comes everyday telling me what to do next and it feels like you are not doing anything for Christ. You are wrong in so many ways there are things you can do in your community your local church, join in a YMCA youth group, and a camping group. When spring time comes, you can go to the beaches and share God in their sporting events that are coming up in your city. Just go out there, do it, and one of these days that voice will come to you saying, "This is the one for you, the gift from God, you finally find it, for others it takes a little more time to come around." And now, tell them this how can a person know God in his infinite glory, you have to talk to him on a daily ongoing basis, praying, reading your Bible. Talking to him and learning to hear his voice don't waste the grace you have. You have to be itching to tell someone about Jesus you must be going through a lot. I think you have been slacking on the spiritual side of things I think the devil drops a virus into your plans now; it's getting personal, trying to get you and your family doing other things. Time to fight back and let the next level of God's power overshadow you, now with me. The devil tries to bring up my childhood, and till this day it is still with me and I know that I am not the only person that had a childhood problem. It got to be hundreds, maybe thousands, or maybe a bigger number than millions adults are fighting with in them selfs. No that Jesus is carrying every sin on his back but this is one to convents me myself so every move I make he is watching me everything down to my pet sins to. That is why he says, come as you are, all the sins of the world he died for on the cross we cannot push ourselves into depression about all of this. Do you understand me, let it go, yell, scream, cry, and let the real you come out. When writing this to all of you who are reading this different kind of book. I'm letting you into my life, this is not a last will in testament this is real but a new beginning for all of us that is facing something in their lives too. So come with me, though my journey to the next level in God, we came this far, and you are a determined kind of person, you really want something out there, life is not going to give it to you on a silver platter itself now, stop grabbing the handicap sign and putting it on your forehead like that. So

I say, try to do all you can while you are young like giving a
sacrifice of praise. Praise God he loves it when we praise him
and how do you praise him in singing songs that tells of his
gratefulness by opening our mouth giving thanks. Psalm 100:1-4.
says. 1. Make a joyful noise unto the Lord, all ye lands. 2. Serve
the Lord with gladness: come before his presence with singing.
3. Know ye that the Lord he is God: it is he that hath made
us, and not we ourselves; we are his people, and the sheep of
his pasture. 4. Enter into his gates with thanksgiving, and unto
him, and bless his name.

Even if you don't feel like doing so, it has to come from
your heart like I say how many times are we going to hell as
many times it takes, so thank you, God, for not taking the air
from this planet, we do not deserve it, but he loves us so much
that you have to draw the line—holy or unholy—a Christian
or saint or devil worshipper. For these signs will follow you
for those that believe in him, with love, peace and joy. You
see things that you have not ever seen before, you feel things
like you never felt before, love can tear down walls, and
besides that trusting, understanding, unity, is the strength in
your hands why do you want to leave this if you must, come
quickly. For those black sheep of the family, the reneges of
life—where is your spiritual compass going here and there,
with no guides whatsoever, I want God to take me to a place
that I have never been before. When life gets busy and you
feel like quitting sometimes, there may be questions that can't
be answered. Trying to solve a problem may take awhile, the
best thing is to talk about it, that I know deep inside of me.
How I feel about something, I think about it a lot, trying to
find away around it, can be helpful or harmful to me and my
family. This is not only for the teenagers, but also for all of
us that are facing their whole life; something needs to be in
any kind of addictions, it has been a personal ravage to get
back the peace in your mind and body. To set an example for
somebody else just maybe I am the one, God sent me to you
in writing this different kind of book, letters to God I think;
it is the other way around a voice letters from God. It is our
choice to discover him. To live out loud, to speak out loud to

him, for each life must write their own road-trip or journey on your road to Jesus, go somewhere, find your hiding place, just you and your God, write in your journal.

Explain what you are feeling in your soul at this moment give him all of you not half now and the other half later if you are feeling like giving up on your marriage, it was a 50/50 thing, and that is the world point of view a half way thing now in this day and time you have to give 110 percent all of you. I understand that now as I have grown in the knowledge of it; to tell the truth, I didn't know about this twenty years ago. It takes time for you to really get to know that person inside and out, to know who he or she really is. This is what I have observed throughout my Christian walk with God. I do not want to be a bad husband, to know where you came from; you want to improve yourself. I tell you, it takes years in the making to be molded in God's love. He shall fill all the missing parts that have been swimming away from you trying to reach out to them more and more, they are drifting far away from you that unstoppable problem that bill you got in the mail. Trying to love someone that does not want to be loved, for the praying mothers out there, keep on praying, for your child is coming back to you, your sons, and daughters; where ever they may be, with me, I learned discipleship at a very young age, in my early teens while off into my middle teens. I helped my father in the film ministry, showing Christian Spanish movies, going from church to church, and sharing the glorious Gospel of Jesus Christ in Spanish church's, I learned a lot by setting up the movie screen back then, the screen stands up on some kind of fold out tripod style, the screen rolls out of the mental black box folded like a movie poster, you pull it upward and it locks in place, now that's cool. The film machine in cased in a mental fabrics, I think it was green, like a 1950s look; but doing this in the middle of the 1980s, I just remember the hot summer nights, the church windows and doors were open and wearing a suit sometimes man, I was hot; we show films on a Wednesday night and on Friday, Saturday, and Sunday nights too. Setting it up with two film reels: one with the movie film in it, and an empty one, I liked when Dad set up the film into the machine just listening to the film go through it. I think that is why I like going behind the scenes on DVD movies in the technical side of things to keep my mind learning at a young age. Long after that, I went on doing roofing jobs with my dad finding a roofing job wherever we could get it, in any kind of weather specially in the summer times, I got really physically fit at that time after school, sometimes I walk home to meet Dad there, or he picked me up from school. I used to change clothes to go to work with him on a roofing job, and then on the weekends I would help my grandpa on his lawn mowing business; on the side all day Saturday he used to pick me up from my house around seven in the morning we didn't get done until seven or eight in the evening that day, and throughout my youth to work for the things I wanted. I continued to work, trying to make money on the side for other things. Back then because my mother did have a job and my dad worked to but it still was not enough money coming in. And going to school that really helped me through out my whole life today. Going to work really shaped me to be a better person to help someone else. And for those that have been working their whole entire life. I know where you are coming from that it has been taught with the money even today trying to reach out to the older people back in the day things were simple your grandpas and grandmas vs your dad and mom that reached out and taught us all the best of both worlds it is a blessing to me and so forth.

And now in the present time, thirty years later, it has been braking up some families, the thing is they don't teach the kids values and what's wrong and right, we have confused a generation with no values we fail to lay down a firm foundation for the next generation to follow by, I wonder what happen if the tables were turned the other way. Let us see if they don't lose their minds saying it's boring. We have too many things today that are distracting us, from not spending time with our kids and God, and the real you cannot hear from God with an iMusic or iPod in your ears all the time don't get mad with me out there for telling the truth. I know life changes, so change for the better. Oh, please do not shut off yourself, doubting that is all over, all those thoughts running through your mind, all those phone calls in the house—phone calls, messages are filled up with creditors from banks, from the house mortgage, the car payments, and no food on the table but still you have a smile on your face. Time to bring out some fruit of the spirit up in here, which is love, peace, and joy that extra special thing called "praying"; there is only one of you in the world, so how are you going to use it, for bad or for good. You can kill someone with the words you use coming out of your mouth or you can give life to someone that is dying from the inside out. Is it like fighting with two different personalities with you for those who are living by them "self" or living the single life feeling that lonely spirit saying to yourself, "Can I really love a God I have not seen or touched, but I can hear him, You probably can't hear him but in so many ways God, has shown you him speaking to you. His voice is loud, in the middle of the night, calling my name." One big God calling all the names on this earth to come to him at the same time, but you forgot only the selective can really hear him. I am talking about the blood washed, filled with the Holy Ghost, of the spirit they are one the same and fire of Jesus Christ, the people who are Sons and daughters of the living God. Yes, a living God of the universe, not a stature of clay or stone. He dose not hear the sinners prayers because they are not real with him we play our games trying to slack your way around God. In fact we do whatever we won't, the choice is if you want God to hear you now, you better hang up the phone because Gods not hearing it. Really he knows our hearts, praying in vain is void, when he forgives you of your sins that's where it starts repeat do it right now, with all of that said and done, now you can say can you hear now like a cell phone. I saw an infomercial today about a survival kit that had a lot of stuff in it to last a long time, and I was thinking to myself. I think that all the sinners of the world better write down the 1-800 number on the TV screen right now, just in case of a future refinance that you might need to save your life. Romans 3:22-25.says. 22. Even the righteousness of God which is by faith of Jesus Christ unto all and upon all them that believe: for there is no difference: 23. For all have sinned, and come short of the glory of God;

24. Being justified freely by his grace through the redemption that is in Christ Jesus: 25. Whom God hath set forth to be a propitiation through faith in his blood, the remission of sins that are past, through the forbearance of God. Acts 3:18-21.says. 18. But those things, which God before had shewed by the mouth of all his prophets, that Christ should suffer, he hath so fulfilled. 19. Repeat ye therefore, and be converted, that your sins may be blotted out, when the times of refreshing shall come from the presence of the Lord; 20. And he shall send Jesus Christ, which before was preached unto you: 21. Whom the heaven must receive until the times of restitution of all things, which God hath spoken by the mouth of all his holy prophets since the world began. But wait for a second; I think most of you just might take the mark of the beast anyway sell your soul to the devil so that you can keep on living your life like you are already doing in the first place, self-centered and only thinking about yourself shopping like it was no tomorrow. At one time or the other, some of us has or will be blinded to the truth in his or her lifetime. The devil has set a bees nest in your eyes, ears, and brain and given you the same instant replay going around the bush, your entire life. Going through the motions on autopilot, we need to change something in our daily living. Revelation 13:15-18.says. 15. And he had power to give life unto the image of the beast, that the image of the beast should both speak, and cause that as many as would not worship the image of the beast should be killed. 16. And he causeth all, both small and great, rich and poor, free and bond, to receive a mark in their right hand, or in their foreheads: 17. And that no man might buy or sell, save he that had the mark, or the name of the beast, or the number of his name. 18. Here is wisdom. Let him that hath understanding count the number of the beast: for it is the number of a man; and his number is Six hundred threescore and six. Yes "666".

So pray without season and start reading your Bible out of the blue I don't think the devil saw that coming, he is saying to himself what the hell, what's that, he's playing games with you the devil has plans for your future. We need to cut him off he is storing up bad habits for now and then. We are not children of the devil side, we are God's children sent to this earth to tell of him and that we want go quietly. You see, the devil likes to pick us out one by one all by yourself like a fox going after a sheep. We need to come together right now in unity, like going to a Bible study sessions, and going to church and meeting other Christians and going on a group outing like road trip, or what they say in school, a field trip. Formulize like a family outing, set a date and time, and don't break that promise to you are your kids, please cut the phone off stop your business call, your family is your lifeline—to living a long life, so come and plan it the best you can, set it for three months or six months from now. Let time work for you; don't let time pass you by, for you don't get another chance like this. So store it up in your mind because the human brain is so complex, and even the cameras of today try to capture the moment. Like a picture frame, it freezes time in your mind, zooms in, take a look at it for the millionth times again. So how are you picturing your road in front of you right now? Is it fear, being tormented by the demands of your past? And in your present, you are not that kind of people that cries every night, but wait You think somebody is going to take you away for good, not to see your family ever again? Is it something holding you back from pursuing gifts? Is the devil trying to make you kill yourself of feeling hopelessness and letting depression set in? This is not good. This is not a one-day thing; we people are fighting every day for souls, trying to stay pure for God in your own life. Nobody else is so cold and cruel, with no feelings of human life at all in a world. You are alone and on your own, but with God you are not alone. He tells us time after time to choose our road wisely, "My son and daughter, so come as a little child." He says if you come with a willing heart confess your sins before him. Give your life to God.

He does the rest for you; he erases everything you have ever done that was bad. Be true to your God, to your husband, and to your wife, your son, daughter, mom, and dad. You cannot teach this overnight, it takes time over time. To say, there is peace in the midst of the storm that you are facing today. So get out of the bed right now and go do something you have never done before; it doesn't have to be big but small steps. And stop crying, it is going to be all right, and you cannot quit on yourself like that. There are too many of your loved ones that really love you. Call on his name, "Jesus" like a fragrance after the rain saying to yourself what are you doing here is this one of the roads that some people in their everyday life are facing you think if you can blink it away all your problems they will disappear out in thin air just like God can wrap it up in his love of forgiveness keep going on the right road of your destiny. For some people, they are living in a dream world that a tire will go flat someday, and a light bulb will go out when flipping that light switch, or that the birds fly south for the winter, or how God protected you from that accident yesterday or today, Gods grace is with you every day. And for all the drivers in a morning rush hour and also in the evening, and carpoolers, so you get to see a lot of the backs of people's cars, especially the bumper stickers—a lot of stuff way out there, some of it does not make any sense. Well, I think from my stand point that all bumper stickers should say, God bless the road raggers, forgive them Lord for what they may do, pushing ourselves to the limits, getting all stress out, all for nothing making a clear-minded decision. Now what road am I on? Here, I see people running, jumping, walking fast, walking slow on their road. I see them taking their sweet time, enjoying the scenery. Now what's up with that? So you are telling me that all kinds of people from all races, from all kinds of cultures, from poor, middle class, and the rich must have a road to follow.

Asking myself, "Why do I sweat a lot when I exercise?" and that is because I am burning calories and my body has a cooling system in place, so I won't fall out and die. Some people get burnout on their own road, you have to pace yourself step by step like I said in the middle of the book. Nobody has the right to force you. There is a word call a willing heart your free will a person must have the disciple mind set, people have many different ways of approaching life as a chapter, you have your good habits and your bad habits the things you do in the present to prolong your life span right now. Running from something, you feel the sense of fear, and one of these days, you are going to stop that it is going to catch up with you, and now it is a wake-up call. And you are getting angry, and your mind causes you not to think clearly, in doing stuff that you would not think over. These are the elements of anger: You can see it, feel it, hear it, you can touch anger and when you hold that person, she is shaking, scramming, and screaming at you. The one you love is trying to pull away from you. And now what do you do from there? They respond to you in a negative way, so now you respond back in a positive way with love. Now these are the elements of love: You can see it and feel it, say loving words to calm the other person down, if that doesn't work, maybe just leave the person by himself or herself alone for a while, until they cool down; for some, you got to attack life in a different way some times.

"Oh God," I do not know what to do from this point of my road, it is a lot, all kinds of stuff lingering in my mind so many files so many choices I would like to connect all the good roots to the bad roots in all one setting in my brain, could it be that. I maybe delaying my blessings from the Lord, it does feels like that, is it on hold for awhile like a lay away plan stored away but can't get to it. Paying on it, now how bad do you want it? So you pay more for it to get it out quicker. I wonder asking this question to God, "Does a blessing from you have and expiration "date"? Am I too late to get it or not, I put more pressure on myself taking in a meeting with myself I wonder will this hurt me in the long run this shortcut on my road, by choosing that I might be putting more road to my travels." The time is going too fast right now, when you are getting older, by the year, I know to speak for myself, well it was true when we were kids. Time seem to slow down, I am not saying to you that this is happening to you right now, it may be that you are standing in your window—a small one, medium one, or a big window at your office, home, or maybe you are sitting in a city bus, on a train, in an airplane that has a great view of the earth, or you maybe sitting in a taxicab, seeing all the people walking about. And a school kid day dreaming, looking out of the school window, what are you thinking about is it the future I think the future is looking inside from the outside and not us looking from the inside looking outside it has to be you making the first move on this having a future in the standings. So what are you doing there? Trying to figure out what role should I play to stand on while you are thinking about that, be yourself, and if something clicks with you, the people will hang around, it is with the coworkers. This is all because of the light of Jesus shining in you. So go ahead and don't be afraid, let the lord take control of you. For your sake, you are not that kind of a person to follow bad role models, especially all the famous pastors that like to be seen, maybe you don't like to hear this part but the world has famous people too: movie stars, the music stars, the rap stars. We pay millions of dollars to see them on the stage and on the big screen. I am not trying to get famous I am guided by him the lord Jesus Christ you can not be in the world, saying my light is shining before men, you can be in the world, but not of the world.

Oh wait a minute can you hear lighting coming from heaven on this one, I tell you this, there is coming a time where there is going to be some cleaning going on in some body's houses what is the real truth about the under the table special that will be brought to light. Reform, my foot! Why are we still paying more taxes more than ever, we need to tear down the walls of separation, here in America? I need the real Christian to come out, come out wherever you are, time for a awake-up call here. We all know that the devil's time is almost up here, trying his best to deceive and affect people's mind and heart and trying to take the soul of man for his gain. God changed my life when I was six years old I went though some changes. When my dad got me from my real dad you see he wanted to adopted me. So he is my dad now, and my real dad he was around he didn't want to marry my mom so my mom was blessed with someone who wanted to marry her they mate in church. The other family did not win the case. I was living with my mother at that time she was a single parent for several years, until she met my step dad, they went on to get married in 1979 and now we all are still here in 2011 I wouldn't be here without them, they changed my life, as of today it has been a long road for me and my family. I have one Brother Daniel and 2 Sisters Deanna and Anna, my brother-in-law; Ben Parker is a great guy. My family is very mixed. My father is from Monterrey Mexico, my mom is black and all my family is mix, my brother-in-law is white married to my older sister, Deanna.

I just wanted to share my world with you; you have to teach your child about family and to love all races and about Jesus at a early age. They are going to need it. It will save you fewer problems for the parents, but still you are going to have a lot of bumps in the road each child is different. But we are still learning new stuff every day. It is worth showing our kids that Jesus loves, us and that he died for our sins. The real you will never give up on life. Are you fighting with this with in yourself when you go to bed at night or is it the opposite instead in the morning? Do you think God is testing you? To see how far you can go, he is not forcing you to talk to him, just giving you a warning, when was the last time you really talked to your maker, quit being so stubborn. Put down your cell phone, the laptop, the iPod or iPad, and the Wii video game. We need to stop sitting on our butts and put some frequent flyers miles and time to hit the knees; no more pushing buttons, open up your arms, free your hands, and lift them to the sky and start praising God. We do not know when we are going to die. So please start being nice to people all year round, even on the holidays. I think some things need to be said in this different kind of a book. The people need to see the words in print, some stuff has never been said. I know that I am not the only one out there, but I want to send a message to everyone out there. Now this is my side of the story of walking on this road of life the road less travel.

You should ask yourself, "What makes me different from the other person?" Well first, I am a Christian a newborn person, not a green horn. I have been a radical Christian for a long time now, seeing the same reflection of myself changing to an older, wiser person. Let me see the only mirrors. I see about three mirrors a day—in my house, bathroom mirror, my car mirror, and the public restrooms. There are all types, shapes, and sizes of mirrors, the kind that shows the real you outside. You saw something you did't like at first but what you saw was the fake you so you already knew yourself by heart in a bad way. The devil likes to jump in some places. He is not supposed to go there that is forbidden, trying to stop the clouds in your mirror, cutting you off from your life source "Jesus." While walking on your road, try setting a goal for yourself. Here comes a cloudy mist stopping you from seeing your way. And here comes the darkest hour of your life, not watching ahead of time and not praying your way through the problem. This is when you hear God's voice will show you the way, that no weapons formed against you shall not prosper it want work, if you fell God get right back up he will never leave you are forsake you.

Come as a little child before him. I do not know what's going on after this. If I get the first chance to motivate you, save you from yourself and things of your flesh or the last chance to speak to you in these words. I hope I helped you through your trials and tribulation. Maybe you have a child in the hospital, keep on praying Mom and Dad the lord is a healer to them who will have the faith to believe, or maybe you are going through foreclosure on your house, just may be God let us walk together for a little while. 3 John 1:2 Says this. Beloved, I wish above all things that thou mayest prosper and be in health, even as thy soul prospereth. To get you a head start on this road but there are no shortcuts, just remember that he is cutting you like a diamond, fine-tuning you for your own journey. Now it is your choice to look at yourself what state of mind you are in right now. Are you mad at yourself over your own road mistakes maybe you are comfortable where you are right now, you found yourself screaming at the sky which is blue today in all its splendor but you keep on cursing yourself day after day.

Don't care anymore. Now how are you getting yourself out of this one? Your friends and family said that you are the ugly duckling or the missing link of the chain. No more roller coaster life, and not thinking your life is not worth living. Yes, for me, you mean so much more than the things in life which gives us a really good slap in the face. In this life you will get scared up physically and emotionally in your soul to, we need to rest this body when we been though long fiery trials so every move you make god is watching, sometimes he steps in just in time when you need him, this may sounds funny to you it is the truth in most cases. Just sit down somewhere in your house or apartment, were ever you may be, just close your eyes if it is safe to do so, and just let the spirit of God talk to you, also let him mend your Broken heart. Let the tears flow, he is making you a happier person. Treat yourself the right way and come back. No more hurting your family with a bad attitude. I know that life changes, and you have to move on with your own life understanding and putting God first and then yourself. Puts things in balance, it should go that way. Do you want to walk a mile in my shoes? Just to show you the way, the kind of thing's, we try to feel the void in our life, a major event that happened when we were kids, growing up in a poor family, trying to find work, living off welfare system, trying to pay bills, and as a single parent taking care of two kids maybe four or more help is coming for you. In the day you are stuck needing a job, and you have regrets concerning some bad choices stuck in the mud in the middle of it all. A past regret is what that is, so life goes on. I say that there is an end to a problem, short or long term, you got to find out how to end that problem soon as possible just put on a good old thinking cap if you can find it now you have a bat in your hands now that's your ideal and then step up to the plate and when that problem come your way hit it to the left field and when a curve ball of life comes hit it with a home run behind it.

God sends it the best way, going on the right way, so keep a song in your heart, please try to live a stress-free life your road is connected to you. The real owner is in your DNA, if you stumble across somebody else's road, trying to be like them, then somebody is going to get hurt very bad in the process. Why people want to send their own selves to hell? It is like suicide it's a soul thing here, people don't think their is a hell their is, and some body is going there if they don't live right. Revelation 21:8 .says this. 8. But the fearful, and unbelieving, and the abominable, and murderers, and whoremongers, and sorcerers, and idolaters, and all liars, shall have their part in the lake which burneth with fire and brimstone: which is the second death. No more talking about it, start making plans to getting your life "right" now just do it. No more last chance sin acts playing with fire just putting yourself out there. Like daggling meat, hanging from a tree limb and wishing that the wind, don't blow you away, that the devil is like a roaring Lion seeking whom he may devour. Look in 1 Peter 5:8 for this reference. Smelling you quick as possible in the blowing of the wind, to blowing your cover, saying to yourself, "Can I really beat the devil at his own game." Just to mention God is watching you. If you have a good heart or not, the bottom line is "quit sinning" and that is the best thing you can do for your soul right now. So tell me if I am right, when all the things of life have gone from you. What then? The next best thing is to grab a hold on God; he is your lifeline for this because it is the right thing to do, your ticket to heaven. How do we know that we have it inside of us with the natural eye? We can't see it; we feel it, this is getting close to God. It is, the way to God during our lives and sometimes it is unscripted and unrehearsed that's called somebody throwing in a monkey roach into your program. Fighting off sin where do we draw the line between you and God, saying how far can I go with God. What kind of person would do that kind of thinking you minus well say "God" I don't want you in my life right now. Are you crazy you are looking for a early grave. I want to be ahead of the game and not behind it. Oh God, show me the way how to love people to see the real me, the way you want me to, take me to that place in you God, looking at yourself in the mirror every single day. Do you like what you see or don't like what you see? Sitting on your bedroom floor with only a bed, a desk, and a lamp, can you beat your own rap with your own confessions? You see, time is passing really fast these days now. To me, when you are the oldest you see a lot of other things that the other brother and sisters did not see, one of them was that I got to see my mom and dad when they were younger and to see them now thirty years later we have grown together a lot. Just looking back in my life while in my present, knowing that the forties will be knocking at my door pretty soon here, we all are racing for time, keeping youth in clear view at our grasp. Can you really slap yourself every day of the week about this, or other problems that you have? So stand up from your chair, fix your pants up, smooth out your dress, take a couple of deep breaths of air in and out, and let your heart and soul guide you. It is not your mind that plays with emotions; it is your heart, you need a clear sense of it, is it worth the fight you must do. I fight for my soul and the actions of my words.

Jesus is the one, who can and will show you the way, and what you are looking for, Jesus can be your pal, your best friend; you can talk to him anytime, anywhere if you have the key. I have the right to praise God in my world. I say that the Word of God is sealed in my heart, and the air I breathe right now is what he gave me, to speak that into existence what to say and speak taking a leap of faith here and talking about making your move that chance of a life time on God not on yourself, give up self and you must, while you are young. Hebrews 11:6 says this. But without faith it is impossible to please him: for he that cometh to God must believe that he is, and that he is a rewarder of them that diligently seek him. Growing old without any regrets; oh God, show me the way home. What is your life right now? Is it in the past or present or just putting some things in your life on hold, the clock is ticking on your dreams? Psalm 23:1-6 says this. 1. The Lord is my shepherd; I shall not want. 2. He maketh me to lie down in green pastures: he leadeth me beside the still waters. 3. He restoreth my soul: he leadeth me in the paths of righteousness for his name's sake. 4. Yea, though I walk through the valley of the shadow of death, I will fear no evil: for thou art with me; thy rod and thy staff they comfort me. 5. Thou preparest a table before me in the presence of mine enemies: thou anointest my head with oil; my cup runneth over. 6. Surely goodness and mercy shall follow me all the days of my life: and I will dwell in the house of the lord for ever. We must push the bonders in our innermost being telling the flesh to stand back bring in the real self the new man and woman of God. All that bad stuff you did for fame, and riches, and when all that went, you were stripped from everything you own, even the clothes on your back, you wanted to hear the

barer truth you got it. So you came into this world naked; you will leave this world naked you can't carry anything with you when you die, your soul go's back to God the body will return back to the dirt. 1 Corinthians 15:50-57says. 50. Now this I say, brethren, that flesh and blood cannot inherit the kingdom of God; neither doth corruption inherit incorruption. 51. Behold, I shew you a mystery; We shall not all sleep, but we shall all be changed, 52. In a moment, in the twinkling of an eye, at the last trump; for the trumpet shall sound, and the dead shall be raised incorruptible, and we shall be changed. 53. For this corruptible must put on incorruption, and this mortal must put on immortality. 54. So when this corruptible shall have put on incorruption, and this mortal shall have put on immortality, then shall be brought to pass the saying that is written, Death is swallowed up in victory. 55. O Death, where is thy sting? O grave, where is thy victory? 56. The sting of death is sin; and the strength of sin is the law. 57. But thanks be to God, which giveth us the victory through our Lord Jesus Christ. God is not looking for the lukewarm Christians; he is looking for the hot Christians who are faithful no matter what happens, and letting your enemies realize you have a backup, the lord is on your side no eye for an eye here, let God handle it, if they take anything, but they cannot take way your family. Because he is a mighty God full of power and will show him self strong. Now tell me what is the common sense about all of this right now in America? Is that the world viewpoint or a Christian viewpoint almost like saying there is peace here on earth and there is no more fighting going on. So what is next for the human race? We need the Bible and God as our wake-up juice for the soul. Can we find the common ground to save a person's life in the physical body in that same regency the some act for the soul? Jesus is authorized only to give you peace, love, and happiness to freely give salvation to anybody who asks. He is not a racist, because he made you in his image; come as you are and do it, you will be blessed and give God the glory in all you do in this life. I leave you with this Bible verse, and *God bless you.*
ON THE ROAD LESS TRAVELED: THE ROAD WARRIOR

Psalm 37:4-9,

4Delight thyself also in the Lord; and he shall give thee the desires of thine heart.

5Commit thy way unto the Lord; trust also in him; and he shall bring it to pass.

6And he shall bring forth thy righteousness as the light, and thy judgment as the noonday.

7Rest in the Lord, and wait patiently for him: fret not thyself because of him who prospereth in his way, because of the man who bringth wicked devices to pass.

8Cease from anger, and forsake wrath: fret not thyself in any wise to do evil.

9For evildoers shall be cut off: but those that wait upon the Lord, they shall inherit the earth.

And Home Is Where the Heart Is

By Anthony Ruben Lee

CPSIA information can be obtained
at www.ICGtesting.com
Printed in the USA
LVHW112239010821
694291LV00004B/194

9 781456 874063